DBA Transformations

Building Your Career in the Transition to On-Demand Cloud Computing and Extreme Automation

Michelle Malcher

⟨IOUG⟩
independent oracle users group

Apress®

DBA Transformations

Michelle Malcher
Huntley, Illinois, USA

ISBN-13 (pbk): 978-1-4842-3242-2   ISBN-13 (electronic): 978-1-4842-3243-9
https://doi.org/10.1007/978-1-4842-3243-9

Library of Congress Control Number: 2017962867

Cover image designed by Freepik

Managing Director: Welmoed Spahr
Editorial Director: Todd Green
Acquisitions Editor: Jonathan Gennick
Development Editor: Laura Berendson
Coordinating Editor: Jill Balzano
Copy Editor: Karen Jameson
Compositor: SPi Global
Indexer: SPi Global
Artist: SPi Global

Distributed to the book trade worldwide by Springer Science+Business Media New York, 233 Spring Street, 6th Floor, New York, NY 10013. Phone 1-800-SPRINGER, fax (201) 348-4505, e-mail orders-ny@springer-sbm.com, or visit www.springeronline.com. Apress Media, LLC is a California LLC and the sole member (owner) is Springer Science + Business Media Finance Inc (SSBM Finance Inc). SSBM Finance Inc is a **Delaware** corporation.

For information on translations, please e-mail rights@apress.com, or visit http://www.apress.com/rights-permissions.

Apress titles may be purchased in bulk for academic, corporate, or promotional use. eBook versions and licenses are also available for most titles. For more information, reference our Print and eBook Bulk Sales web page at http://www.apress.com/bulk-sales.

Any source code or other supplementary material referenced by the author in this book is available to readers on GitHub via the book's product page, located at www.apress.com/9781484232422. For more detailed information, please visit http://www.apress.com/source-code.

Printed on acid-free paper

Every day amazed at how my girls grow and I am so proud. Thank you, Amanda and Emily.

⟨**IOUG**⟩
independent oracle users group

About IOUG Press

*IOUG Press is a joint effort by the **Independent Oracle Users Group (the IOUG)** and **Apress** to deliver some of the highest-quality content possible on Oracle Database and related topics. The IOUG is the world's leading, independent organization for professional users of Oracle products. Apress is a leading, independent technical publisher known for developing high-quality, no-fluff content for serious technology professionals. The IOUG and Apress have joined forces in IOUG Press to provide the best content and publishing opportunities to working professionals who use Oracle products.*

Our shared goals include:

• Developing content with excellence
• Helping working professionals to succeed
• Providing authoring and reviewing opportunities
• Networking and raising the profiles of authors and readers

To learn more about Apress, visit our website at **www.apress.com**. Follow the link for IOUG Press to see the great content that is now available on a wide range of topics that matter to those in Oracle's technology sphere.

Visit **www.ioug.org** to learn more about the Independent Oracle Users Group and its mission. Consider joining if you haven't already. Review the many benefits at www.ioug.org/join. Become a member. Get involved with peers. Boost your career.

www.ioug.org/join

Apress®

Table of Contents

About the Author ix

Foreword xi

Chapter 1: Types of DBAs...1

Where Do DBAs Fit? 3

System DBAs...5

Application DBAs..8

Automation DBAs 10

Next..12

Conclusion 12

Chapter 2: The Set of Skills 13

Technical Skills 14

    Platform Specific 14

    Testing and Implementation 17

    Installs and Upgrades 17

Soft Skills..17

    Communication 18

    Documentation 20

    Relationship Building (Interpersonal Skills)...............................21

    Adaptability...21

    Organizational 22

    Leadership...23

Conclusion 25

Chapter 3: The Future State of Databases 27

Technology 30

    Storage 30

    Data 31

Disruptors 32

    Technology..33

    Social Networking 33

    Security 33

    Virtual Reality, Augmented Reality, and Artificial Intelligence.......................34

Many Platforms..35

Database as a Service 36

Databases in the Cloud 38

Conclusion 41

Chapter 4: The Database Machine Administrator (DMA) 43

Exadata Database Machine..44

Appliances 46

Cloud Engineered Systems 47

SuperCluster and Other Servers 47

Architecture Decisions...48

Automation...49

DMA 50

Conclusion 51

Chapter 5: Cloud Database Administration...53

Type of Clouds...53

Tasks 56

Tools...59

Capacity Planning 60

    Discovery 61

    Workload and Data Analysis 62

Security 63

Migrations 63

Application vs. Cloud DBA 65

    DBaaS DBA vs. Cloud DBA 67

Conclusion 68

Chapter 6: Database Security 69

Security Teams 69

    Building a Team 71

    Security on DBA Team 72

Security Planning 72

Reducing Risk 74

Cloud Security 76

Auditing and Reporting 77

    Automation Security 78

Addressing Vulnerabilities 79

Security Learning 80

Conclusion 82

Chapter 7: Data Professionals 83

Data Quality 84

Data Integrations 88

BIG DATA 89

Conclusion 91

Chapter 8: The Art of Automation **93**

Tasks 94

Dependencies 96

Automating Test Plans...96

Conclusion 98

Chapter 9: Change and Cloud Therapy............................**99**

Job Satisfaction 100

Cloud Therapy 101

Change Management..104

Work–Life Balance 105

Skill Development 106

    Test Environments 107

    Life Learner 107

Conclusion 108

Chapter 10: Creating a Transformation Plan **109**

Transformation..110

Evaluation 112

New Skills 113

    Planning..113

    Acquiring 115

Mentoring..115

What Stays the Same...116

Not Just a DBA 117

Conclusion 119

Index...**121**

About the Author

Michelle Malcher is a database professional with a vast knowledge in database environments and security, developed from her 17+ years in this field. She is a well-known volunteer leader in the database and security communities, with roles as Independent Oracle User Group (IOUG) past president, and as a Fuel Founding board member. Her deep technical expertise from database to development, as well as her senior-level contributions as a speaker, author, Oracle ACE Director, and customer advisory board participant, have aided many corporations spanning architecture and risk assessment, purchasing and installation, and ongoing systems oversight, including large financial institutions. Michelle is currently a security architect for Extreme Scale Solutions.

Foreword

A book like this has been a long time coming. Being a DBA is not an easy calling – especially in today's world. There was a time when DBAs were prized keepers of data within organizations. What we did was a mystery to most, but the role was somewhat predictable. With the introduction of IaaS, PaaS, SaaS, machine learning, big data, and artificial intelligence, the role of the DBA has markedly changed. No two days are even remotely alike, and it seems the rate of change has accelerated beyond what most of us can comfortably cope with.

Everything evolves and the role of the DBA is no different. What separates those who thrive and feel energized from those who feel defeated, is whether one sees opportunity or dreads the tsunami of change that is upon us.

Michelle is not only a brilliant technologist, data security expert, and recognized author – she has also lived the life of a DBA for many years, and witnessed the dramatic change in the data ecosystem. Michelle's book describes what the DBA of the future might look like and how to achieve success. For the first time ever, data has become a strategic resource in many organizations, offering a competitive edge if it is mined appropriately. While this poses many questions and raises concerns, it also provides immense opportunities for the DBA. No longer is the DBA responsible for mundane, predictable work; a whole new world of data (not database!) management has opened up that is fluid. The DBA role is now no longer rigidly defined but it must be co-created to incorporate many facets of data management. It is no longer about the technology, but about the enablement of business and strategy through technology.

I have had the pleasure of calling Michelle my friend for years. Michelle and I were introduced to each other through IOUG when we were both DBAs so we 'get' it. This book may surprise, startle, and energize you to grasp the future, whatever that looks like. One thing is for certain – you will become a better DBA as a result of reading this book. I will leave you with an important question to reflect on as you read Michelle's book: what type of DBA do you want to be?

—Maria Anderson

CHAPTER 1

Types of DBAs

My story might be like that of many Database Administrators. I started off in database development. I have not met too many DBAs that have started right out of school as a DBA, and it seemed normal for the DBA to come from development or infrastructure teams.

Database administration is not necessarily a first technology job because of the vast knowledge that is needed about databases, infrastructure, development, and even the business. Agreed that there are also beginning level DBAs that are part of the team or mentored by someone, and now with some of the technology advancements and features of the database, it is possible to see people starting on this path. The other question is if the DBA position was chosen by you, or did the position pick you? The accidental DBA or volunteered DBA probably received the job because the position was not able to be filled and with some additional training, you found yourself in that role.

It seemed like a good opportunity, especially to work with the various infrastructure and business teams. This is a major reason for my decision to move over into that role. Not only were you a significant part of many applications, but the database continued to advance and develop new features to support those demands. It was an environment that provided challenges, change, and constant learning. Relationships needed to be developed with the developers and the business to be able to support their needs. The infrastructure teams became our allies as we built systems to install the databases. Being in this role allowed me to learn about many areas in technology and refine what was needed for business requirements.

© Michelle Malcher 2018
M. Malcher, *DBA Transformations*, https://doi.org/10.1007/978-1-4842-3243-9_1

The skill set of the people to manage the databases and help teams get business data in and out quickly has been important in business. However, there are discussions with databases and infrastructure going to the cloud about whether DBAs are needed. Are we accidentally going to become Cloud DBAs? Or is there a different path where these skills are needed in an area that will provide different opportunities? This is not the first time that DBAs have had this discussion about transitioning, and if the role was even needed. It is also not the last time, but the goal here is to give direction on what the world of databases will bring as well as the surrounding environments of security, data integrations, and cloud. A view of the current state of the DBA will help us understand this transition.

The DBA job is not always clearly defined. Do the databases support the application development? Are they really part of the infrastructure? What about all the moving components from database options to just backups, and where are the lines between operating system to application code? There are some definite gray areas when it comes to defining what DBAs do. It might not always be even understood between teams. I believe that it might even be blurrier in the future. There has also been a shift in different database platforms too because of how they appear to be easier to install and build up and tear down in a development environment. Notice I did say appeared to be easier. This is critical in understanding what can be provided by the database and making sure that the right database is available for the job. DBAs can assist in these areas, but I will discuss that more in a later chapter.

I remember first supporting table changes and migrations for the development teams. I was also responsible for backups because how could I make those changes without the proper backups first. Other times there were just the system tasks of backups, restores, replication, server builds, and installations. There were also other components that played a part to that with high availability and disaster recovery. On the other side there are components for performance and tuning with partitioning and material or snapshot views.

Where Do DBAs Fit?

Organizational placement of the DBA probably gives the first clues as to what the tasks are for the DBA. Placement in the organization can show whether a DBA is going to be more system and infrastructure support, or work closely with the application teams to build and develop applications. DBAs can also be found on data services teams that can provide more insight around data management than around the database itself.

The organizational chart in Figure 1-1 shows that there are two branches that DBAs can be found under. The CIO branch contains database teams with the infrastructure teams. This doesn't necessarily mean that all they will do was the infrastructure work, but where they are organized as part of the enterprise.

The CTO area should have more of the application direction and will find that the DBA teams work more with the developers and manage their teams with the database teams. DBAs can find themselves in groups or as an individual in these teams. But they seem to have been organized by tasks that they normally perform.

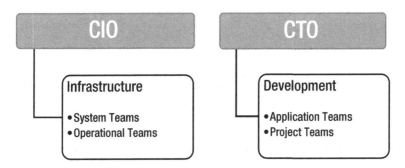

Figure 1-1. *Organizational chart to find DBA teams*

Along with the thought that it depends on their tasks, a data services team that functions as the DBA team can act as if they are under the Chief Data Officer (CDO). This is even a fairly new branch of enterprise and not all companies will even have this group. They tend to be your data management, data analytics, data integrations, and basically anything data focused. They sound like a perfect group to partner with as the guardians of the data. Another branch that is getting even more popular is the Chief Security Officer (CSO). The DBAs might be in the administration role or in the security engineering role under the CSO to make sure the databases are secure.

The newest group to join in as to where DBAs can fit in an organization is the Chief Cloud Officer (CCO). The databases are going be part of the cloud solution, and this would make sense as they are either supporting the cloud infrastructure or the data that is in the cloud. The organization might be like that shown in Figure 1-2.

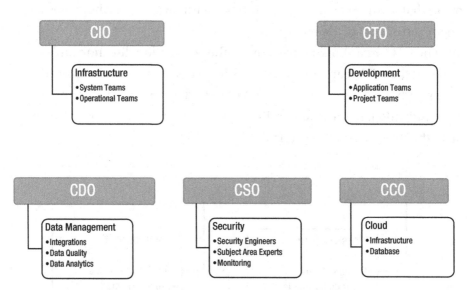

Figure 1-2. *New Organizational chart to find DBA teams*

The following chapters will talk about the different opportunities for a DBA to transition into several of these roles. But to transition into a different branch of the organization as a DBA or a database engineer takes justification. Transitioning varies by organization and what structures they already have in place. Even without some of the services or groups, transitioning doesn't make it impossible to start a group, just a little more creativity is required. The point is to be in a group that makes it easy to communicate to the teams you need to work with and makes it clear what role you are playing. It would not make too much sense to be in the Data Management group if all you do are database installs. The different alignment will be based on how the group can get the best requirements, communication, and delivery of the databases.

As you can see from the different alignment of the DBAs, it might have made sense to have a centralized group under the CIO. But now with the diversification of the DBAs with skills and focus areas, it seems reasonable that there will be smaller groups of DBAs throughout the enterprise. The question will be whether they are still called DBAs or have transformed into another title. Movement in this direction demonstrates understanding of the business needs and how they are using data. It allows you to be a valuable part of the team to drive solutions and utilize the data assets.

After seeing where to find the DBA teams, let's look at the different types of DBAs with their tasks so that we can move forward with the future transformation. And we can dive into what changes there are for the DBA from the current focus because of the databases and infrastructure we deal with, and a future state with database as service, as well as other services – cloud and even more data coming our way.

System DBAs

The team that is called in to increase the amount of storage to the database, or to restore the database or probably most importantly to patch and upgrade the database is most likely made up of system DBAs. System DBAs have the main task of taking care of the database infrastructure and the actual database instance. The configurations include database options, parameters, and features of the database.

With Oracle 12c the system DBAs are going to be taking care of the container database (CDB). They will be creating the pluggable databases (PDB) and performing cloning and migrations of the pluggables as necessary. Depending on if there is a security team handing access, system DBAs will be adding users for the PDBs or at least monitoring the privileges. The storage will be part of creating the PDB and making sure that there is proper capacity for the PDBs in the CDB. The development of Oracle 12c naturally separates out the tasks of the system DBA from the application DBAs. Microsoft SQL Server also provides this separation from the database instance and the user databases.

Note   High Availability options can split up System DBAs even more in managing cluster services, Automatic Storage Management (ASM) instances and data guard management. It depends on the size of the environment, but these roles allow for separation of duties or still part of the system DBA team.

As we look through areas that the system DBAs support, keep in mind the skills and knowledge it takes to support tasks in these areas. Skills are going to be discussed more in the next chapter.

- **Infrastructure**. As part of their job function system, DBAs are performing the database creation and software maintenance. They have access to the database servers and managing the processes, file systems, and software binaries for the databases. They will be looking at server and network performance and verifying that the database processes are all working as expected by reviewing the alert and system logs.

- **Storage**. Planning of capacity includes server resources and certainly storage. With ASM, management of disks groups and allocations to the databases and tablespaces can be part of an ASM administrator role, but more likely this falls into the skills of the system DBA.

- **High Availability**. Making sure that the databases are supporting a 24x7 environment means that cluster services and Real Application Clusters (RAC) are part of the installation, configuration, and patching jobs. As the environment scales out provisioning servers and maintaining the cluster and performance, there are tasks that need to be addressed. Data Guard and standby servers are part of the maximum availability architecture and become the responsibility of the system DBA.

- **Manageability**. Monitoring of the database servers and verifying that all the components of the databases are available are under management of the systems. Even after installs, the work for patching, upgrades, monitoring activity, and performance are needed to ensure a stable environment.

- **Recovery**. It is not enough to just back up databases, but to plan and ensure that databases can be restored. There are other features of the database that allow for this besides backup and restore, such as flashback and failover. Recovery testing and planning for failover are included in these responsibilities.

There are, of course, tools that can assist in these areas and we will discuss the future state of the databases and the possibility of managing many of the databases as one and simplify these processes. Tools and standards are essential for the system DBAs, and they need to understand more than just the database, as they also work on the OS, networking, and storage.

The system DBAs support many database servers and provide a highly available and stable database system. They have the skills and tasks to install, deploy, and maintain these environments and provide normal maintenance tasks, storage allocations, and backups.

Application DBAs

Application DBAs are going to understand more of the application processes and data to support the business and developers. Instead of looking at the system processes and the availability of the database, the focus of application DBA is on database objects, data flows, and application performance.

PDBs are going to be the environment that the application DBAs find themselves in because the user and application objects and activity will be in PDBs. The application DBA does not work in isolation, and instead needs to work closely with system DBAs and application development teams.

Data modeling is another role that these DBAs will have as they assist with the application development. Some of these roles can be separated out into different teams and functions depending on the size of the organization and sensitivity of the environment. For example:

- **Database Objects.** Modeling of the tables and database design for the application and assisting in writing scripts for the application code. The objects, including tables and procedures, can be developed to be part of the unit testing of the application. Planning of indexes and views can add value to the development teams.

- **Performance Tuning**. Tuning the database code
  and implementing solutions for performance issues
  are responsibilities of the application DBAs. Here
  again, working with the system DBAs to coordinate
  activity of the database with application and database
  code is very useful for troubleshooting. There are
  skills here of working through issues, benchmarking,
  and understanding the workings of the database.
  Recommendations for indexes, database options, and
  parameters come out of tuning practices.

- **New Features**. Besides the new features on the server
  side, normally there are database code and object
  enhancements. In understanding the application
  and what they are executing, the new features can be
  matched up to reduce development time or provide
  other benefits with performance. Constant learning
  with the new features and working with developers to
  understand gaps, problem areas, and requirements is
  one of the many challenges for the application DBA.

- **Migrations**. Moving data from production to test
  for development might be a system task or for the
  application DBA to make sure that data is masked
  properly and refreshes happen regularly. Another
  migration is object code to production. This might
  be an operations task, but getting the code ready,
  reviewed, and tested is for the application DBA to
  handle.

- **Data Management**. Data movement in production
  environments with data APIs to other systems is part of
  data management. Data workflows and how to get the

needed data from one database to another is where the application DBAs have the knowledge of the different environments to provide the right way to move data or verify that there are data APIs available. With data management, there is more work with the CDO group or even other business teams.

Note   DBAs are not normally the owners of data unless it is data about the databases. They are considered the guardians of the data. They can assist the other teams in tagging, classifying, and performing data quality steps but would not be the first group for data definitions and tying it back to the business.

With skills in data modeling and movement, the application DBAs work closely with the development and application teams to ensure the data is available and protected. All types of DBAs must continue to work with each other, communicate well with other teams, and continually learn about new features to implement in the databases.

Automation DBAs

Isn't everyone supposed to be looking at automating processes and reducing manual efforts? Well, yes, they are. However, there might be tasks being performed as a one off to see if it works as needed, and then it can be handed off to the automation DBAs to include it in the processes. I would expect that these DBAs are working heavily in Oracle Enterprise Manager or Oracle Cloud Manager. They would have a scheduler tool to coordinate jobs and writing the wrappers around code that will automate what used to be one-off tasks or manual ones.

Automation DBAs might be part of one of the other teams, but this is a type of DBA that will look to make sure that the jobs are running as scheduled and implement processes around the maintenance and data tasks. They work to keep everything a smoothly as possible and that there is little manual intervention in production. Taking tasks from development and automating it would be the responsibility of this type of DBA. This can be the team that gets handed code from system and application DBAs to manage and automate. Verifying that code is running as expected and the jobs are executing would be in reports reviewed and audited from the automation DBAs. In separating this out, the separation of duties allows for handoffs from development to production and reduces the manual issues that can occur.

- **Scheduling**. A schedule might be a simple thing, but realize that there are maintenance, data, ETL, and application jobs that might need to be coordinated. The scheduling of these tasks can be tricky so that they do not collide or slow down any of the production environments.

- **Code Automation**. An automation DBA can have code that will wrap around tasks for automation so they can just plug in jobs. They can review other code to make sure the jobs are doing what they are supposed to do. They are looking to automate processes and workflows whereever possible. Automation of reporting should be under their responsibilities too.

- **Monitoring**. Monitoring the execution and errors on the databases, the automation DBAs can report on timing and that the code is being maintained properly. Also in monitoring, they can find other opportunities for processes and work with the other teams to make sure that these tasks get rolled up into the automation.

11

The automation DBA can help enforce standards with processes, code, and database structures because automation is simpler if the standards are dependable. The skills here are to understand what processes can be automated and to take requirements from others to plug into the automation tasks. The understanding of the database activity and being able to write and maintain database code allow them to complete their responsibilities around automation.

Next

There might be other types of DBAs that have been developed for other organizations based on demand of tasks and types of applications they might be running. These are typical types of DBAs that are part of the current state of the environment. A couple of times I hinted to what is coming next or to pay attention to the skills that are being developed while working as one of these types of DBAs. The question is what is coming next, because there needs to be some sort of transformation since databases are obviously changing in where they are installed, how they are being managed, and an overall technology shift to service like and cloud systems.

The DBA must take the skills from these typical areas of focus and know that the expertise developed here is vital to continuing to support the databases even though the landscape of how and where it is going will be changing, if it has not already.

Conclusion

Before we start the transformation process, let's look at the skills we can pull out of the current state DBAs as well as some other important skills and knowledge that will allow us to move forward in a world of cloud computing and automation.

CHAPTER 2

The Set of Skills

Calling all technology people who like to have control over the environment. That could be most us, especially if we are DBAs. It is difficult to confess that you became a DBA because you like to have control over the data and who, how, when, where, and what happens to the data. I will speak for myself here, but you are welcome to join me in that statement if you so desire. Anyhow, some of the best skill sets can also be a weakness in dealing with a transitioning role, which we will work through in Chapters 8 and 9. It is difficult to give up or perceive that we are giving up something that we enjoy and feel is a very valuable set of skills. The great news is that most of the skills and knowledge we have as DBAs can help us become even better DBAs and be used as leverage to move in a different direction.

As we went through the types of DBAs in the previous chapter, I hope you were thinking about some of the skills that are needed in these different roles as they are going to be our baseline skill set that we have as DBAs. Depending on the opportunities, skills can always be developed and improved. And with some of actions and activities that we do, the syntax is not the skill that is being sought after. It is the skill to google the right version of Oracle or the database to get the correct syntax that is important.

Relationship building is a must for allowing DBAs to be able to work with all of the various teams. This is not always something easy to accomplish as there are challenges with communication, resources, and different priorities between the teams. It is a skill that can be mastered with practice and learning effective communication.

We can break down these skills into the technical skills that are still required for any changes and transformations, as well as the soft skills that absolutely must come with the changes.

Technical Skills

The technical skills are going to vary to go along with the types of DBAs. Having spent time in the different groups will continue to round out the skill set. Having worked with the application teams gives more of an application understanding and provides coding opportunities. The technical skills that are needed to administer databases are different than coding full applications, but there is quite a bit of code that can be database specific. The DBA is not necessarily the one writing the application, again pointing back to the separation of duties, but to understand how to read through and interpret code helps with working on database development.

Platform Specific

There are database platform-specific skills such as Data Guard and RAC and even some performance tuning. Even different versions of the database can require additional knowledge, such as CDBs and PDBs. Of course, there are database core skills, just changes in syntax, which are needed for any database: backup and recovery, object creation and modification, and monitoring. Patching and upgrading databases follows similar processes, plans, tests, backups, and executes the plan. Table 2-1 shows a list of the core DBA skills versus Oracle-specific skills.

Table 2-1. *Technical skills Core vs. Oracle*

Skill	Oracle	Core	Comment
Backup/ Recovery		X	Different syntax and possible options, but backup and recovery needed for any database
Export/ Import		X	Data movement and extracting data and inputting data
Database Maintenance plans and schedules		X	Analyzing indexes, validating objects
RAC	X		
Cluster Services		X	
CDB/ PDB	X		
Installation		X	Always should read the files with the installation
Patching		X	Notes to apply patches
Performance Tuning		X	Need to understand some specific database platform rules and query plans to implement solution but process to tune the database similar
Troubleshooting		X	Know where the error logs, alert, and system logs are to provide information
Capacity planning		X	
Storage		X	
ASM	X		Disk groups, ASM instances, and tablespaces

(*continued*)

Table 2-1. (*continued*)

Skill	Oracle	Core	Comment
Network/OS		X	Connections to the database and working on Windows and Linux/Unix platforms
Disaster Recovery		X	
Active Data Guard	X		
Data Modelling		X	Need to be able to model objects. Just indexes, tables, and coding features are different
Partitioning		X	
Query Tuning		X	Not just parameters and indexes but tuning the query to perform well
Stored procedures, triggers, views	X	X	Oracle has PL/SQL and where you might use a trigger in Oracle or function, it might be a procedure in another platform
Security	X	X	This is general here, but it will be expanded in Chapter 6.
Monitoring		X	Monitor activity, performance

This is not a complete list for all the databases, but it is a significant list providing good detail about the tasks and knowledge that would be needed. Most of these are core database skills with differences in code or options that would be available.

Testing and Implementation

A technical skill that might be overlooked is testing and implementing unit testing. Developing test plans is part of the development code for the procedures, tables, and validation of the processes. There is skill in integrating the database testing with the application code. Plugging in code and details about the objects will get you validation before going to production.

Installs and Upgrades

Technical skills have been what you have been practicing as a DBA. The technical side of performance tuning and implementing high availability systems might be the coding areas that you really enjoy doing. It is good to know a skill that will always be needed. The DBAs that really enjoy installs and upgrades is in a good position because with changes to the cloud, these skills will need to be transferred over also. Even the Oracle has been simplifying the install and patching processes. They have announced a couple of times over the years with releases that the database is easier to set up, configure, and manage, but the technical skills of the workings of the database, and how to use the features for other processes are the technical skills to possess.

Soft Skills

DBAs, whether we wanted to or not, have developed soft skills along the way. We have had to communicate with other teams, plan very large environments, and make the connections between the business all the way down to the OS and servers. There are not going to be opportunities to work in isolation. As a DBA, there are opportunities to lead in changes and development processes. Even with security, the DBAs should be educating and leading with practices for protecting the data in the database systems.

The soft skills are something that can be worked on, and it is a constant personal growth opportunity. As our soft skills improve, it is not just our work lives that benefit but also our personal lives outside the working hours. An SQL query may not matter to our family but better communication does. Volunteering for the user community and other organizations provides a safe environment to practice these skills. Sharing our technical skills in written or presentation format keeps the growth going.

Communication

Communication means more than just talking with others. This requires understanding the audience and detailing with issues, requirements, and expectations. Agreeing with and planning and then turning around and ignoring the priorities is very poor communication. There is a reason why I list communication first: because the better we can communicate what we do and the work we can do, the easier it will be for us to be in a position where we enjoy working, feel challenged, and know that we are adding value because of the communication we give and receive.

In the world of emails and Instant Messaging or text, we have developed another way to communicate that is not as formal, and we can pull in others that may or may not be needed in the conversation. There are already several books written on communication, business communication, even how disruptive miscommunication can be. Any time spent improving how we communicate with each other, including writing effective emails is well worth the time.

There are a couple of areas in which I feel are extremely important to have great communication skills.

1. Develop communication plans that can be used as part of any change or project. The communication plan would include how to get the audience and how to communicate so that the details are

specifically stated. The plan should include what the reason or issues are for the communication, why it is being stated now, what the call to action is, and any other expectations or details that belong with the message being delivered. A standard template is usually the best way to do this because it makes sure that all the pieces of the communication are included and it is recognizable by others.

2. Understand the audience to provide the right details. A more technical email for other engineers and more high level and key points for management (they can always ask questions if they want some technical details) would be appropriate. This can also apply to sending emails back and forth in which the audience may not have been part of other discussions or meetings and questions should be asked to understand what they need or what they are asking so that details do not get missed.

3. Communicate an agenda for a meeting. It is very easy to get off track or not know what the meeting is for, so the agenda helps and allows others to be prepared. Sending out notes afterwards captures the highlights, which makes it easier to track; fill in others not attending; and believe it or not captures what the time was spent doing, which is useful for timekeeping, year-end review, and management briefs.

4. Notify of changes and project milestones. There is probably a change process, but there might be additional information to educate and deliver other meaningful information to the developers and applications. This should be part of the communication plan, but it might be going to smaller audience first or even management as this is being decided upon.

To show the importance of the communication, three out of the next five skills depend on it. This is a skill that you probably don't know that you have been using, but examine how you are communicating, look for ways that it is currently being used, as it is a skill to bring with in any transition.

Documentation

As DBAs, we have read a ton of documentation or at least, more than we can count, the release notes. It is a skill that some of us find easier than others to write but we all do it in some fashion. The details of what is being executed, how and why, in documentation format for others to understand the details of the system for others to support. We create runbooks, detailed information about our set of scripts, and the databases with configurations.

DBAs tend to document the owners of the databases and application owners as we use these in communications about the environment. Chances are that most of these details are in a database but we can pull reports and use the information for other processes.

Documentation is normally created to outline steps for installations, upgrades, and health checklists. Test plans are also documented with plenty of test cases to have the successful upgrades and installs. Needing to know how to restore a database, the DBA of course has documentation of scripts and steps, including the logs from the last practice restore.

Data flows and database objects line our walls as we work to understand the data model and internalize all the intricacies of the application and how they are using the data. This information equips us to provide the optimal support for the database system.

As data flows become more complex with the cloud and other integrations, this type of documentation along with processes will be needed in future environments.

Relationship Building (Interpersonal Skills)

The good news is that we are dependent on working with others because the databases need servers, network, and other infrastructure. The data also comes from the business and application teams. It does also make it challenging to have to coordinate and work peacefully with these teams, but the DBA teams seem to make it happen.

Communication is key to building these relationships. I find it easier when expectations are set properly and any changes are communicated as quickly as possible. Other teams respect that and start to work closely with the DBAs because they get honest answers and details as things happen.

DBA teams can assist in making connections with other teams and serve as a liaison either to application teams or infrastructure teams. This also comes from understanding what it takes to keep the system running along with the business requirements and SLAs. This knowledge can translate into reviewing SLAs and requirements for cloud infrastructure too. And it provides the needed education for the business to validate they are meeting their demands in the cloud architecture.

Adaptability

The DBA might not appear as one to adapt to new environments because we have carried a toolset along with us for many years. However, the toolset can and in many cases has been updated along the way to account for new features and changes in how the database performs. As we went through the technical skills, the core items for databases has not changed much over the years, but how to effectively run those tasks and adapt to the new features for completion of these tasks.

Many of the manageability options of the database have become part of the internals of the systems, which have been automated, but in understanding the workings of the environment we are looking for the next issue. There have been many times that a script or monitoring has found something new to look for, and we add that to our arsenal.

We are already not the same DBAs from 10 years ago. We have adapted to new OS, new database platforms, and virtualization. These shifts to our environments have developed our abilities to shift and adapt to how we configure and administer the databases, even include other platforms in the data flows and integrations.

The continuous learning that is part of the excitement of being a DBA has encouraged us to move along with new options and add this variety in the tool belt. Even with some of the old scripts we remember how the processes have functioned and now can adjust and keep moving forward with the small and major shifts.

Organizational

Welcome to control freaks anonymous, where we have organizational skills. This is a skill that most DBAs possess and are very proud of. Nothing wrong with that, especially since it is absolutely needed to manage all the databases, processes, activities, and users.

We stay organized to make sure that gaps are being covered and that steps are being followed to ensure repeatable processes. The organized steps can be tested, repeated, and reused for other areas too. It is rare that a DBA really has a one-off process, because chances are that it will need to be used again. It could be administration tasks or performance-tuning steps, but repeatable processes are typical for the databases. Organization is used for this because it follows a specific flow; you cannot backup a database after starting the upgrade. It's too late at that time to restore. Having a couple of backup or rollback plans is normal for the DBA.

Being process oriented and organized allows you to think through the details and then execute them. In reviewing architecture designs and discussing different infrastructure, DBAs can ask several great questions to help get to gaps or figure out what is missing in a process to make it work. These questions come from the understanding of the processes and being organized to know what the order in steps should be. Organizing questions to evaluate new environments, plan cloud migrations, and prepare data integrations are future skills for the DBA, which is a soft skill that we are already possess.

Leadership

Leadership is not about a position, because we are not all DBA managers or team leads. We have databases that we manage and teams that we work with. We lead with our skills and knowledge in that we contribute to provide database systems that support the enterprise.

We are proactive or decide to work toward that goal. We lead in this way instead of being reactive, even if it can be difficult at times. Modifying what we do to work in a way for standards and being able to provide answers before being asked is a goal and can lead in the right direction. There are opportunities with future direction to lead other DBAs and prepare for moving databases to the cloud or other services. Understanding the benefits of these moves and providing explanations to other teams will lead the changes. The transition to another type of DBA is using these skills and will challenge us to grow them.

We have presented information about new features, storage capacity, and hardware choices. Not only are these communication skills, but they demonstrate how we lead in our area. Without the discussion about hardware and database improvements, we would be falling behind the curve.

We lead in the areas of making our environments better and current to provide what is needed in the enterprise. These are details that allow us to talk with management to be proactive with our environments.

As DBAs, we are passionate about databases. We are driven by goals to have a secure, stable, highly available database, and we are protective of the system to keep it tuned as we have planned. As leaders, we should be sharing this with others, mentoring other administrators and developers to understand and appreciate the databases. This passion can carry over into other areas that we are serving and allows us to lead with example as we approach the new database world.

In building teams we have DBAs exhibit leadership. The team-building effort flows over into what happens in the database. It inspires us to learn and become even better in our talents and craft, and pass it along to others. Let's look at a few leadership qualities in building these teams that will be needed in transition:

- **Mentor what inspires us**. We are passionate and inspired by people around us in the database profession. Share that passion. Share the reasons for enjoying this profession. Explain why and use that to inspire others.

- **Team building**. Putting together a team is not easy, and they need to work together to achieve the goals. Building a team means to be using the different talents of the individuals to work for the benefit of the team. It will make a stronger team. In building a team, it is also worth looking into what happens with the team when things change. If goals change or the direction of the project and system, the team needs to work to adapt and continue along the new path.

- **Team goals**. Defining the goals might be related to the current projects and activities or what the team needs to become for the environment. Individuals might have goals to continue to learn, advance in their careers, and be able to add value in the team. Team goals need to include all of the individual members, and it might take working with each one to understand the goals and where they fit into the picture. The goals of the team should be apparent and discussed how to obtain. Goals to shift the database environment to the cloud or migrate to different a platform should at least be planned as a team; even if not everyone agrees with the goal at first, they can agree with the plan to achieve it.

- **Developing skills**. We have been discussing technical skills and soft skills, and leading will not only be developing these skills in yourself but also helping others to see what skills need attention. There is always something more to learn and work on in these areas. In teaching and mentoring others, we actually learn more.

Conclusion

Technical and soft skills have been developed over the years as a DBA. The technical skills have allowed us to support and maintain the mission-critical database environment effectively. They gave us the understanding of the internals and how the database applications function. We have learned from application owners and developers the requirements and how to implement them. The communication, leadership, and other soft skills are going to be critical for moving forward, assessing the direction to plan for, and making the change.

CHAPTER 3

The Future State of Databases

Relational, Graph, NoSQL, Columnar, InMemory, Warehouse, and Analytical databases are all part of the database administrator's job. The database platforms continue to grow and develop. Even with many relatively new databases now part of the development and production environments, the relational databases still hold a large market share and purpose.

With the collection of even more data on a daily basis and new uses in companies for data-driven results, the various databases serve in the processes and system. Data growth is one constant for the future. With all of the social media channels, smartphones, and Internet of Things (IOT), data is predicted by several different sources to grow to over 100 zetabytes in the next 5 years. This is just an increase from just under 10 zetabytes in 2015. Not to mention that there are advances in technology that can even drive this higher. Artificial Intelligence and plenty of IOT sources might even make this more than predicted.

© Michelle Malcher 2018
M. Malcher, *DBA Transformations*, https://doi.org/10.1007/978-1-4842-3243-9_3

Quote   "The Data Warehouse is far from dead, it is the core of any business reporting system, but it must adapt faster. We generate significant data through our business applications which feed the traditional data warehouse. Businesses will adapt their data warehouse architecture and finally see a widespread use of Hadoop for landing data." Ian Abramson, *Predictions*, IOUG Select.

The Data Warehouse is far from dead, as it is the core of any business reporting system, but it must adapt faster. We generate significant data through our business applications that feed the traditional data warehouse; 2017 will see businesses adapt their data warehouse architecture and finally see a widespread use of Hadoop for landing data.

Can you even how much data is going to be in your data center or cloud databases in a few years? The database professional does have their work cut out for them to maintain these very large environments. The data and information business is going to be booming and bringing in significant dollars to the industry. The business of data is not going away anytime soon, and there will be a role for the guardians of the data.

In Figure 3-1, the chart shows the growth of data coming from mobile as forecast by Cisco Virtual Networking Index. The data is planned to grow to 49 Exabytes per month from currently around 11 Exabytes per month. This could be the result of more video and pictures, but it is data that will be coming from devices that can find itself in databases.

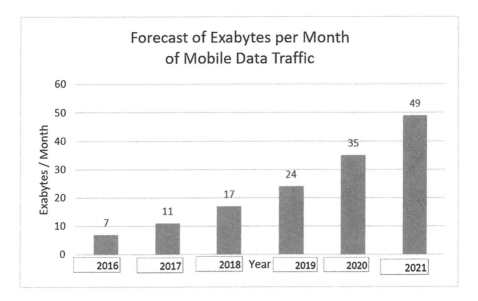

Figure 3-1. *Forecast Monthly Mobile Data Traffic. Source: Cisco Visual Networking Index: Global Mobile Data Traffic Forecast Update, 2016-2021*

Additional interesting information coming out of this forecast from Cisco VNI is the number of smart and non-smart devices and connections. The number of non-smart device connections is decreasing even though they continue to grow in the forecast. However, they will still be growing year over year by significant amounts. Figure 3-2 shows the chart with this information about the number of smart devices and non-smart devices. With the increase in devices and connections, the data will continue to growth. Through online shopping, photos, and other social media, the data growth is supporting the importance of the database.

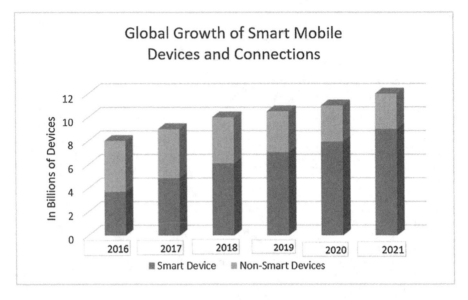

Figure 3-2. *Forecast Monthly Mobile Data Traffic Source: Cisco*
Visual Networking Index: Global Mobile Data Traffic Forecast
Update, 2016-2021

Technology

As seen with the development of the smart devices influencing the
forecasts in the mobile devices, other technology is affecting how we
manage databases. Virtualization changes how we look at resources and
servers. Provisioning of new resources is more transparent and available
with growth or peaks of services. Server technology continues to advance
and using it with virtualization allows for using these new technologies.

Storage

Oracle Exadata engineered systems provide servers that are specialized for
Oracle database workloads and configurations. These engineered systems
are a good example how the technology is keeping up with the database,

high availability options, and features. The performance with the storage and configurations allows for the databases to run as they are designed. Memory options and parameters are working for the In-Memory database of 12cR2 and other configurations bring in the new features as they also enhance with each release of the servers, either with upgrades or new components. This actually limits some of the intervention from the DBA and the server hardware. Supporting these engineered systems is a task that a Database Machine Administrator (DMA) would carry out. We will discuss the DMA in Chapter 4.

With the amount of storage, the hardware is critical to make sure to be staying up from the latest trends and technology to improve speeds of disk operations. Solid State Disks (SSD) are going to be what is being used along with flash. The spinning disks are going to be a thing of the past, and new innovations will allow for more data in memory and faster data access.

Data

The type of data is changed too. With Augmented Reality (AR), Virtual Reality (VR), and Artificial Intelligence (AI) videos and pictures, larger datasets are being accessed and stored. With AR and VR traffic, data access per month will be reaching 160 Pedabytes up from 16 PB, according to the Cisco VNI Forecasts. AI might be the unknown as many are just touching the surface with the ability to make decisions on very, very large datasets. It can surpass the forecasts if there are new opportunities in this area.

Data collected from wearables, sensors, and other IOT devices are going to collect data and expand the amount of data crossing through the data center. Even if you think about how much data you currently use on your mobile devices each month and how that has changed over the past couple of years, just imagine how quickly that will change in the next few years. It will definitely be well over the 4GB mark, unless you have teenagers, which make it soar above 10GB very quickly.

The devices are advancing with the wearables and what is being collected, costs for points of entry decreasing, and the technology for other devices are going to play a big factor on how quickly the amount of data grows and changes the forecasts. Technology in the data center will need to be enhanced at speeds to keep up with the demand. The life cycle of devices is changing from what it was several years back to be five years, down to three, and probably now between two and three years. The technology and devices are keeping up with the business and end users.

Technology is driving both sides of the equation with devices that collect the data, and the servers, storage, network and other components to support the business with the data that flow through. Databases are going to store the necessary data for business processes and day-to-day information as they also need a way to process data and the workflows from Big Data streams to integrate with the systems.

I might be getting ahead of myself in talking about the data streams and integration as this is a place where DBAs can transfer into, but the technology of the devices and support compounds the data growth and the opportunities for the DBAs. This is going to be considered as several technology game changes for all kinds of information that is available.

Disruptors

Disruptors are innovations that potentially create new markets and new value. Therefore, they are disrupting the current markets and values in the market. It is not just something shiny that grabs our attention for a moment but it is something that disrupts, interrupts, and moves us in a different direction because of that advancement or innovation that can't be ignored.

Technology

Technology is a big disruptor and will continue to be going forward. We just finished talking about how technical devices and how they are going to continue to provide more data and information. These are a disruption to the database environments as there are capacity plans that are extremely different now than they were a couple of years ago and will be very different in the future. Accounting for the new data market, the IOT data collection is going to add to business value as long as we incorporate how we are handling the data disturbance and manage these changes.

Social Networking

Social Networking is a disruptor as businesses are using these forms of communication as a marketing outlet, or information gathering opportunity. This is now becoming part of the plans in the business, but they might not have been included before. With the younger generation using this as their way of communication, this will also disrupt the business and how they not only market to them, but how they also prepare for them to join the workforce.

Security

Security is a disruptor in that it causes current progress on projects to stop and deal with the situation at hand. It might be a new zero-day exploit or a new security patch that has been released and should be dealt with as soon as possible. Breaches cause disruption in projects as they might require an assessment if the right controls are in place and how the environment is handling the possibility of a breach and reducing the risk. Innovations on the hacker side of the equation is not a positive outcome for the market but it will definitely cause a disruption in how it is being addressed and the risk involved. Much more will be covered in Chapter 6 on security, but understand that it is going to be a disruptor now and in the future as the security landscape is going to be one that is always changing.

Virtual Reality, Augmented Reality, and Artificial Intelligence

Mentioned in the Technology Section, VR, AR, and AI are all disruptors as there is constant innovation happening here. Robots that can now perform tasks to provide products more efficiently to the market add value. AI is starting to open new doors on how devices and behave and react, possibly even creating new environments that we might have dreamed about or only have seen in Sci-Fi movies and TV shows. We actually look at some of the movies and think, could that actually happen? Is that real? Self-driving cars are already out there being tested, but what is the next technology disruptor coming our way? It is definitely fun to think about how we might be working in a few years. Already there are plenty of companies that opt for working at home possibilities because of cost savings and technology to support this type of environment. It would be amazing to see VR play a part in going into the office in a way to speak with our coworkers and avoiding the commute.

Why are disruptors even more important now to database environments and the transformation of DBAs? Databases are normally considered a sustaining technology. Yes, it has changes and upgrades, but these are incremental improvements and efficiencies that normally take place. They are not always the innovations that are changing the direction, markets, or value. However, as described above, these innovations in technology and other areas are creating the interruptions to normal business and need to be addressed sooner rather than later. As DBAs we need to evaluate these disruptions in our database environment. Is it going to add more value? Do I need to change the way I am doing things to address it? These honest questions are going to be more than just a simple change. It will be changing and causing disruptions of our current projects and processes if we look at all of the innovations in technology and embrace those in the database systems.

We will see even more disruptors and many of these will influence the database arena. It will change how and what data is collected and the growth. These systems need to adapt and incorporate as needed by the business. This is just the beginning of some DBA transformations as more will happen with new disruptors.

Many Platforms

DBAs support multiple platforms of databases. There are many enterprise-level databases that include types, like relational, key-value and column stores, and graph databases, each with a purpose. The market share of these databases has changed slightly over the past 10 years, but relational databases still make up about 89% of the enterprise market share. Figure 3-3 shows the market share of each of the database platforms based on Gartner and other market research from 2016.

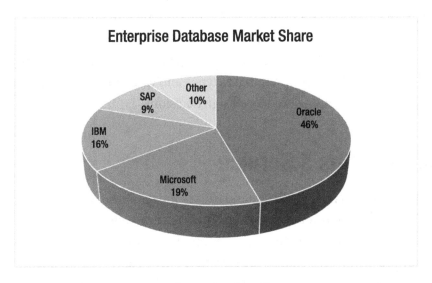

Figure 3-3. *Enterprise Database Market Share*

It is not just Oracle, but MSSQL, MySQL, DB2, MongoDB, PostgreSQL, Hadoop, neo4j, and other platforms that will be found in the enterprise supported by DBAs. New databases are developing as part of cloud services, and the data that is being collected by devices. For example, Amazon Cloud database, SimpleDB, recently emerged as part of the cloud services. DBAs are needed to administer the various databases, and help plan which workloads are appropriate for the type of database. Administration changes for the different platforms and integration between the platforms will pose different issues and challenges.

Future needs of databases are not just based on data needs but can be on application development needs. According to a StackOverflow survey in 2017, developers have ranked databases in order of preference to work with and MySQL is the most popular database. SQL Server, PostgreSQL, and MongoDB are next on the list. This is not to say that the developers have the ultimate choice for the databases, but the reasons they are popular are for ease of use and to work without too many blockers. A self-service model would influence a preference among other factors.

Database platform no longer matters to the DBAs, as they are responsible for managing and administering several different platforms. Understanding the various databases types and when best to utilize them will provide the input needed for design decisions.

Database as a Service

Database as a Service (DBaaS) standardizes the database installation, configuration, and monitoring. DBaaS puts in the needed configuration with security, compliance, and management tools in place with self-service provisioning. It makes the environment scalable with managing many databases as one because of the standardization. DBaaS has database containers that are deployed for the application users. It keeps production and development environments in sync with the same containers and provides services to manage and do tasks and development as needed. DBAs are needed to provide input into the containers for the company to meet policies and expected compliance, but as the containers are constructed and implemented, the DBAs become more focused in the application space to provide management of user objects, performance tuning, and application development.

The containers are developed in virtualized, Docker, Ansible, and other containers. This is a growing trend to use these tools and as this provides a consistent deployment of the database software, database, and configurations. It is a measured service that allows for resource pooling for providing for growth and scalability. Figure 3-4 shows the design of this model, using Application Program Interfaces (APIs) for providing actions that can be performed against the containers. APIs support the on-demand service of the databases to run without additional interaction. Since the databases are deployed and created the same way, it is simple to measure and understand usage. This supports other important parts for database environments such as capacity planning and monitoring.

Figure 3-4. *Design and Advantages of DBaaS*

APIs are going to be an important part of any database in the future. This is the way to interact with databases in DBaaS and cloud environments. It is a standardized way to get data in and out of the database and perform actions and management items. As we will discuss about the Cloud DBA, there are ways to work on developing the APIs or using the APIs to integrate to other environments. The APIs make it so that the databases can be managed as one with the consistent access to all of the environment.

DBaaS can be considered a private cloud environment as it fits the same components of delivery and offers the service to deploy database containers. The future of the database will have databases in containers to deploy either in the enterprise data center or in the cloud. According to a 2016 IOUG Survey on Database Cloud, the growth rate of DBaaS adoption is to triple in the next couple of years. The survey focused on how DBaaS is becoming mainstream and the Oracle Multitenent is providing the required structures to use the containers. DBaaS and Cloud database will probably become interchangeable going forward, understanding that there are several services available that will be part of the offerings that are in public and private cloud environments.

Databases in the Cloud

The major enterprise database companies are investing in the area of the cloud. Companies find value in using the cloud. It might be using the software and applications that are provided, or even the infrastructure to support public-facing applications. It is also possible that cloud supports development environments to cut costs in the test and lab areas. As seen in Figure 3-5, the RightScale 2016 State of the Cloud Report confirms that most companies are already invested in the cloud, both public and private.

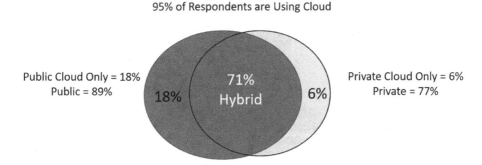

Figure 3-5. *Use of Public and Private Cloud in the Enterprise. Source: RightScale 2016 State of the Cloud Report*

Understanding that database containers (DBaaS) will support the significant growth of cloud environments is vital to the transitioning DBA. Amazon with the SimpleDB has invested in the space of storing data in the cloud, Microsoft and IBM are doing the same with offerings in the cloud and in NoSQL databases. Oracle is building on its cloud service. Flexibility and cost seems to be what they are talking about as Larry Ellison, CTO at Oracle, announced recently that Oracle offers an on-demand service from applications to infrastructure including database in between. The same feature of the Oracle database 12cR2 includes InMemory, Security, and using the Oracle engineered machines on the back end. He talks about simplicity and how it is easy to manage the consumption of the service. The autonomous database that will be completely self-driving is coming to the Oracle Cloud and so will automation of the database with less interaction from the administrator or others. Talk about a disruptor for the DBA and how we manage databases. This is where the transition of the DBA to different areas or even cloud DBA will be the direction. We will cover the Cloud DBA in Chapter 6. Here it is important to understand that with the database providers' investment in the cloud and companies shifting workloads there, the cloud is here to stay. Figure 3-6 shows the transition starting in 2011 and predicting future growth in the IOUG Cloud Survey.

IOUG Survey
2011 compared to 2016

2016

- Significant Increase in Enterprise Data in the Cloud
- Triple the Growth over the next 24 Months
- Enterprises Storing their Sensitive Data in the Cloud
- New Technologies Help with this Migration
- Hybrid Environments for Cost Mitigation

2011

- Private & Public Cloud Adoption up 30%
- Cloud Services Carrying Larger Workloads
- Most Expect Savings with Cloud Deployments

Figure 3-6. *Shift into the Cloud. Source: Databaseas a Service Enters the Enterprise Maistream, 2016 IOUG Survey on Database Cloud, April 2016*

The cloud offers Infrastructure as a Service (IaaS), Platform as a Service (PaaS), Software as a Service (SaaS), and I am sure there will be more services to come. It does appear that there will be less for the DBA to do in the database with the containers and automation and with initialization of the containers and which service needs to be implemented. There are several areas to consider and design questions to ask for migrations and management in the cloud.

The competition of the cloud providers will continue as they innovate and create services that will support customers and their business needs. Figure 3-7 clearly has AWS growth rates far ahead of the others, but each one does have various offerings that should be considered. The database transition to the cloud will continue and DBAs need to be ready to administer these databases with APIs and other tools provided. It is not going to be the same tasks, and looking at the data integrations or other aspects will be a direction to consider for future opportunities.

IaaS, PaaS, Hosted Private Cloud – Q1 2017

Worldwide Market Share
- Amazon AWS over 30% market share with average annual growth rate
- Next is Microsoft with just above 10% market share and over 80% annual growth rate
- Oracle has about 5% market share and 65% annual growth rate

Figure 3-7. Cloud Providers. Source: Synergy Research Group

Conclusion

The future state of the database brings more data than even imagined 20 years ago when large databases were 50 GB in size. Cloud is the future direction and we already need to be planning for our roles. We will continue to have complex environments in dealing with several database platforms, but we can navigate the knowledge and skills that we have DBAs to embrace the future of the database as it is also transitioning.

CHAPTER 4

The Database Machine Administrator (DMA)

The Oracle Engineered Systems and other appliances are creating a new subclass of DBAs – the Database Machine Administrator (DMA). The DMA will be working with the hardware, storage, and OS of the machines. This might be viewed similarly to a system administrator, but because it is specific for machines that will house databases and machines that are designed for databases, the knowledge of the databases is valuable. These engineered systems are also not typical standard hardware and other administrators will be looking to the DMA to handle everything from the database, OS, network, storage, and server needs.

There are new systems and appliances that will continue to be added to the offerings so this will not be a complete list but instead provide guidance on what a DMA has as responsibilities.

Note Even though the Engineered Systems come preconfigured, they need DMAs for specific configurations and server administration.

© Michelle Malcher 2018
M. Malcher, *DBA Transformations*, https://doi.org/10.1007/978-1-4842-3243-9_4

Exadata Database Machine

The Exadata is Oracle's first database engineered system to market. Since then it has had a few different changes and releases. These enhancements keep improving the hardware and features of the database. The OS and database do come preconfigured. Storage is available and the InfiniBand internal network fabric for connections between the servers inside of the Exadata. There are currently two different machines with storage expansion, and they have several different ways to purchase the machine for the current need and expand for growth.

The three areas that are going to be more specific to a DMA are OS, storage, and the network. OS is going to be Linux and with maintenance and monitoring, being able to work in Linux is a must. Storage configuration is going to be configured by the DMA for use with ASM and the file system. Network is for the connections to the internal servers and configurations for Real Application Clusters (RAC).

The DMA is going to perform many tasks that point back to the Systems DBA that we discussed in Chapter 1. The database parameters and configuration, backups, and high availability options are going to be supported by the DMA. Some system changes and patching is going to be handled in coordination with Oracle as these releases are specific for Exadata. Full control is given to the DMA, and they have access to all of the resources in the Exadata. Even though the DMA needs to make sure that the changes, configurations, and coordination happens with Oracle, they do not have to work as closely with the other OS, server, storage, and networking teams. These systems are all contained with the DMA having to manage the full server.

High availability options need to be maintained by the DMA. Knowledge of RAC and provisioning new nodes in the cluster are part of the job, as are using the internal network and being able to configure and manage the nodes in the cluster.

As a DBA, the storage management is normally with the ASM instance. As a DMA it expands further into the device configuration and mappings to file systems and the devices to be used for ASM disk groups.

There is a client utility that can be used to assist in managing the Exadata, exaCLI. This will help in managing database configurations and storage. DBMCLI and CellCLI add to the utility commands for the storage cells.

Transformation into a DMA is a natural step for a Systems DBA. There are a few more areas to learn about with the utilities and managing storage and networking, but the hardware might be the place where it is most comfortable for you, especially if you enjoy RAC, ASM, and having control on the server.

The Exadatas are machines that are engineered for database workloads, but they still provide configurable options. These options are used for performance and security. The DMA must understand how to provide a highly available, maximum performance, and secure environment for the enterprise that owns these machines. The machines are going to be bring into the environment and start using, but without the know-how of what can be configured as the additional benefits for the enterprise might not be available. The same type of understanding for RAC and security with other database servers are needed for Exadata. The advantage is that the DMA is able to make those changes (after a proper testing and change control) but they are the ones in control of the machines.

Along with the Exadatas there are other engineered systems for analytics. The applications can be on these servers, and the Oracle Exalytics is the newest to join the group featuring In-Memory software. These machines are all part of the DMA portfolio. Large companies can have several Exadata machines while others have only one or two. Exadatas can also be used to manage private cloud environments, which may mean there will be more servers coming soon as the migrations to cloud happen. Of course in the large enterprise, there is plenty to do with all of the Exadatas, but the DMA can also support the various appliances as part of the job.

Appliances

Database, Big Data, and Private Cloud Appliances are pre-configured servers. These appliances all require more administration on the database side as well as maintaining the server. Each of these appliances has their own purpose and not having to worry about the initial configuration and software installations takes the guessing out of the setup. It also provides ease of deployment in using these appliances.

The DMA can support these configurations and appliances. Here the knowledge of databases and the OS is needed to provide the proper support for these databases. Again, the DMA can very easily come from the system DBA tasks to support any and all of these machines. Big Data appliances will have other software such as Hadoop and possibly integration tools to work with.

Since these systems, DBA skills are still needed should the DBA need to transform into another position. This is a smaller transition because the database skills of backup, recovery, and high availability are required and then add the storage, OS, and server maintenance work to become the DMA to support the engineered systems.

This is not a book to discuss all of the interworkings of the engineer systems and why to choose one over the other but to look where DBA skills can be used and what systems will need the support in the future. Database servers, appliances, and engineer systems are going to increase their offerings and will need DMAs to step up and be administrators for these systems even if they are in the cloud or Big Data offerings.

Zero Data Loss Recovery Appliance is a recently added appliance. It is for real-time redo transport to protect Oracle databases on-premise or in the cloud. It automates backups to tape from the appliance and off-loads the workload of the backups on the production servers. Monitoring of the recovery appliance is going to ensure that the processes are working and as a DMA, testing restores will be needed.

On the storage side there is the ZFS Storage Appliance. This can provide shared file systems to Exadata, engineered systems, or other servers. This is where more storage and OS management comes to play for the DMA.

Cloud Engineered Systems

The Cloud Appliance is a machine that can be used to create a private cloud offering. The appliance is managed by the DMA and can have mixed workloads. Since this is an appliance, it comes preconfigured with virtualization to stand up a private cloud system in the company's data center. Being a private cloud, it requires someone or a team to manage it in the enterprise. This is more than just the database in the cloud but can also house other applications, and requires understanding of the application services.

The Cloud Engineered System is hardware that is managed by Oracle on-premise. It provides the same Oracle cloud service but on-premise. This means that the data doesn't need to leave the data center, but all of the management of the cloud, Oracle does for you. DMA wouldn't be the ones to ask to manage the Cloud Machine. The Cloud DBA would be handling the databases whether the databases are on a public cloud or on-premise in a public cloud like the Cloud Machine.

SuperCluster and Other Servers

The SuperCluster is another engineered system that varies from the Exadata, but has specific hardware properties that provide additional security and performance benefits. Since this is an engineered system, it is managed by a DMA; however, the OS is Solaris is another opportunity to learn and have another OS in the tool belt.

For private cloud offering, the SuperCluster can be utilized. It is optimized for Oracle database and applications, but is definitely a powerful machine to have access to virtualize for self-service cloud offerings. As we look into private cloud offerings, we will also be looking into more automation and how this will affect the DMAs and DBAs.

Other competitive servers are going to have the same purpose of specific database configurations to provide database infrastructure in the data center. These servers are going to be managed by those understanding all of the backbone of the database: server, OS, network, and storage.

Again, understanding that there are disruptors and new innovation, more servers and cluster developments will continue. There will be new hardware and clusters to manage in the future. Especially with systems that are specific for cloud and database, infrastructures are going to be the challenges for the DMA.

Architecture Decisions

Another challenge for the DMA is significant knowledge about all these offerings and continuing to research any new enhancements. Each of these options has technology, capacity, or placement that will fit different business requirements. The DMA can recommend the right machine for the job. The communication must exist with the business owners to understand what they believe are their needs, and then be able to educate them on options, alternatives to what can drive the future growth, and be the game changer that they are looking for.

Figure 4-1. *Oracle machine offerings*

Figure 4-1 shows the choices we have from Oracle machine offerings. Some of these machines work together such as Exadata, Zero Data Loss Recovery Appliance, ZFS Storage Appliance, and Exalytics Machine. Other machines are options instead of Exadata and they are based on point of entry, workloads, and size of the enterprise.

Design and architecture decisions come from knowledge about the choices and road maps of the systems. The DMA can dive into these areas with the understanding of what needs to be supported and how it will bring value to the business.

Automation

Simplifying the process with preconfigured machines and machines that are engineered for the databases allows the focus to be on other aspects of the environment. There is maintenance and monitoring along with some administrative tasks that will need to be examined for automated processes. Something that is probably executed twice will need to be automated. The jobs for backup, configuration checks, and storage maintenance should be monitored but not day-to-day tasks because of automation.

Another aspect of the automation is understanding that all of these systems should be supporting self-service. The DMA is enabling these services. In providing private cloud and databases access to the DBAs and Cloud, DBAs should be able to focus on their part instead of infrastructure and server configurations. The ability to be the starting point of these services and allow additional automation provisioning and self-service on top of that is a goal and the value that the DMA brings to the environment. Another goal is to assist others in how to provide the services based on features of the underlying infrastructure so that it is not underutilized.

DMA

The DMA is in control of the database machines, from engineered systems to appliances. Providing the administration for these servers means more than just being a systems DBA. There needs to be understanding in critical areas of the systems. They need to support the OS, network, storage, and database.

The main tasks for the DMA:

- Server OS: Oracle Linux, Solaris

- RAC and Data Guard

- Enterprise Cloud Control

- Backup Software (also Recovery Appliance)

- Exadata Architecture and configurations

- Implement Exadata features or other engineered systems

- Storage Cells and ASM

- Network and InfiniBand

- Provide automation on server side

- Support Self-service databases and applications

- Knowledge of server offerings

Conclusion

These are opportunities for DBAs to take system roles into an administrator for the database machines that support cloud, databases, and other applications. The challenges are available to grow into technologies and be involved as these engineered systems provide the backbone for the database environments. DBA transformation into a DMA is an exciting opportunity for the DBAs that find interest in the main tasks and see the value in supporting Cloud DBAs and automation for these systems.

CHAPTER 5

Cloud Database Administration

The question is out there, "if my databases are in the cloud do we need a DBA?" Not a question that DBAs want to hear, but they do want to hear that the answer is, "Yes, of course we still need DBAs." Even with databases in the cloud approaching the point of extreme automation and possible self-healing, the Cloud DBA has challenges in supporting the environment but with valuable database knowledge and insight to the applications, utilizing the data as a needed force for successful cloud database deployment and maintenance.

The last chapter discussed the DMA, which can be identified more with a systems DBA. The Cloud DBA is going to be more associated with the application DBA. With database design, data services, and working with development teams, the Cloud DBA can step in and be involved in these areas and assist by how they can use the databases in the cloud. They can also work on additional data projects because they are not worrying about the day-to-day keeping-the-lights-on tasks.

Type of Clouds

This is not a type of storm clouds or if you see dragons or bunnies floating in the sky, but cloud is a virtualized environment that is specific for deploying services such as Database as a Service. Cloud computing

© Michelle Malcher 2018

M. Malcher, *DBA Transformations*, https://doi.org/10.1007/978-1-4842-3243-9_5

has tools that can deliver these services through web interfaces and applications instead of directly accessing servers.

Briefly mentioned in the last chapter was the idea of public and private clouds. Typical public cloud offerings are through Oracle, Amazon, Microsoft, and Google. These are servers and environments that can handle several different workloads from applications and might just be application servers and also include databases. Private clouds are developed by the enterprise to be kept in the company's data center and the resources will only be shared with internal enterprise users. It is typical that both public and private clouds will be used, along with other servers that might be classified as non-cloud or traditional technology services. Hybrid clouds might have the test environment in a public cloud and production in a private cloud.

Tip   A Public cloud is not in the company's data center, and its shared resources and infrastructure are not managed by the company, but by the cloud provider. A Private cloud is in the company data center, and its infrastructure is managed by the company. A Hybrid cloud has some of both – private and public cloud offerings.

There is a wide range of services that can be provided in the cloud, and they might have been services that were already being provided in a virtualized environment in the data center, which would mean that the shift is not as extreme. An environment that has manual intervention that is not as automated or standardized. As seen in Table 5-1, there are different models and levels of the services in the cloud that can be accessed and used by the enterprise. Cloud DBAs have levels of involvement in each of these models.

Table 5-1. *Cloud Service Models*

Service	Full Name	Purpose
IaaS	Infrastructure as a Service	Bare metal, virtualized computing with networking, storage, and monitoring available
PaaS	Platform as a Service	Resources with OS, network, and storage. Used for application deployments such as databases
DBaaS	Database as a Service	Preconfigured deployment of a database for the PaaS environment. Standardized deployment
SaaS	Software as a Service	Software available via Internet instead of local installations. Office 365 is a typical example

For private clouds the DMA would be working at the IaaS level and creating a platform to provide for a database to be deployed by the Cloud DBA. If a public cloud, then the Cloud DBA would be deploying at the PaaS level and the DMA would be working with other machines in the data center and not involved in this public offering.

At the SaaS level, applications need data access. It might be data in the cloud or on-premise. The Cloud DBA will help make connects to the data and allow for the connections. The trick here is to monitor and make sure that the right connections are being made and only the access from the application is coming through.

Figure 5-1 gives the examples of the servers and the Cloud Clients including the Cloud DBA that performs their tasks using a web browser and other mobile apps. Before we get into the Tools and how to perform certain actions, let's review the tasks of the Cloud DBA.

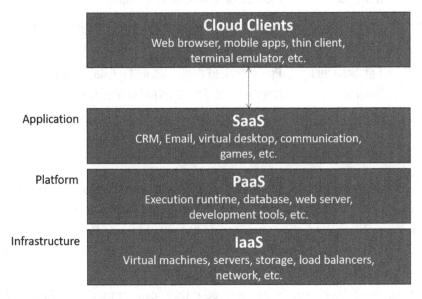

Figure 5-1. *Service Model Examples*

Tasks

Cloud DBAs perform very similar tasks as on-premise DBAs. The database servers, storage, and network are being maintained by the cloud infrastructure team, but the database needs to be administered properly.

The typical tasks of backup and recovery, database object maintenance, performance tuning, capacity planning, and what a DBA is known for needs to be part of the Cloud DBA's list of activities. The connections to the database are slightly different, and access to the server directly is not necessarily allowed (unless it is an IaaS cloud environment).

High availability options need to be implemented in the cloud to provide the 24x7 uptime. This might not be as clear as to why high availability is needed if this is a virtualized environment and should have failover built in, but there are also other reasons to implement RAC for rolling patching or using the option of implementing Data Guard. Recovery through Data Guard and using the high availability options for patching and failover will provide additional safety nets for the databases. Private clouds might have these options supported by the DMA or even the system DBA might support them in the cloud.

With databases in the cloud, they can be implemented using containers. The DBA supports these containers either in understanding the business requirements that are needed to construct the standardized container for each database, or they can create the databases and then administer the databases as if it were on-premise. Figure 5-2 has databases in the cloud that are automated for baselines, features, and options of the database. It is a standard configuration to support monitoring and security. This allows many databases to be monitored as one and provisioning of database based on a catalog and self-service options.

Automation of Features and Baseline Implementations

Standardization of Configurations, Monitoring and Security

Figure 5-2. *Cloud Database Tasks*

The creation of the database in the cloud is a small number of clicks from the catalog, and a consistent baseline database is created based on the options. The baseline will have a set of configurations and security. The cloud DBA can be the one that helps design these standards and baseline, or it can rely on the already developed containers to deploy. It is the understanding that the database being created automatically places the features and baselines in place. This does simplify the implementation of the database, along with the monitoring because it should not deviate from the baseline or standard. Easy checks against the baseline show what is different, and abnormalities are easier to detect for security purposes.

Cloud DBAs are going to be instrumental in making sure that data sets can talk to each other, which means that this is helping applications get the right APIs and restful data sources or helping with connections to the various data sources. Additional data areas will be discussed in Chapter 7.

The tasks that we have listed so far for the Cloud DBA:

- Ensuring Backup and Recovery

- Implementing High Availability

- Creating Databases from Catalog

- Database and Application Projects

- Performance Tuning

- Monitoring and Consistency Checks

Additional tasks that we will take a look at for the rest of the chapter are these:

- Cloud Control

- Capacity Planning

- Migrations

- Patching

It almost seems like a regular DBA job and task list. However, there are more automations and simplified tasks that are part of the cloud environment. Along with these tasks come some old and new tools for the Cloud DBA to use to accomplish them. *The Cloud DBA-Oracle: Managing Oracle Database in the Cloud* (Apress, 2017) is a great reference.

Tools

Oracle Enterprise Cloud Control is going to assist with on-premise and with Oracle cloud databases. On-premise is like the enterprise manager and is called cloud control because of the release. Cloud control can be used for setting up the configurations and provisioning of the databases. It is a tool that is available to connect into database on-premise, in the Oracle cloud, and other cloud environments public or private.

Managing Cloud Control is another way a Cloud DBA can be fully involved. With other tasks simplified, managing of the tools can be taken over to have a well-supported tool. Options that are available in Cloud Control will help with managing the database security, objects, and other parameters and configurations.

The Cloud Control helps with performance with the tuning tools, baselines, and current activity. It allows for management of the various databases that have been provisioned, and it is a tool to provision additional databases. Depending on the access to Cloud Control, the view can show the environment to have the perspective on performance and see where bottlenecks might be. Viewing resources in Control Cloud shows information not only about performance but capacity.

Another tool for the cloud environment is DBaaSCLI. The DBaaSCLI has restful services and APIs for management of a couple of areas for the databases. Some of the tasks are not available the same way. The access to the server is not allowed because it is a cloud environment. This is the tool and service console that is now what is used to accomplish the following tasks:

- Change SYS password

- Patch the databases

- Rotate master keys for encryption

- Data Guard and DR

  1. Check and configure standby database

  2. Switchover and failover standby databases

Other database tools will help in supporting objects, privileges, and data for development and migrations to production environments. Of course, the tools for creating a database are going to be different as it will use the DBaaS user interface or another cloud interface that allows for the database creation.

Capacity Planning

Some of the planning to move to the cloud environment requires capacity planning. It defines the cost of the environment and forecasts growth as planning resources for the private cloud or what makes sense to migrate to the public cloud. Capacity planning means examining CPU, memory, and storage usage and potential growth.

With on-premise database servers, storage planning is to know when new disks need to be allocated, but in the cloud, it is validating that the charges for the public cloud match the resources being used, and that growth matches budget and other planned costs for the databases.

One of many reasons for moving to the Cloud is to be able to have flexible resources. But this does not mean that the understanding of the resources that the database uses is not needed. If an application consumes more at the end of the month, that is not only an opportunity to tune, but an important tracking period to verify that resources are being given since they are needed and that the database is not caged. This is the flexibility of an on-demand resource.

Discovery

As part of the migration to the cloud, a large discovery process might be in order. Discovering the databases that would benefit from the cloud by flexible and on-demand resources, the costs of the data center and maintaining hardware would be valuable information for the baseline of the databases.

Since the cloud is an on-demand environment, others might be creating databases and bring applications into the cloud. The advantage of the cloud is the capture of creation for chargeback purposes. This is where the discovery and capture of the baseline is needed to be able to review the initial costs and demand on the system with the increase in capacity and whatever resources it requires.

If the public cloud is being used, it might require certain consolidation of information of which public cloud is being utilized, details as to offerings that are being considered, and baseline costs with resource statistics from CPU, memory, and storage. The catalog of databases is still a needed tool for the Cloud DBA. The connections and data flows should be simple for the applications and data users, but it is the Cloud DBA that helps make this possible. It is easier if the cloud is in the data center and standardized in a private cloud, but one thing we know as DBAs is that there are reasons for different database platforms and there will be reasons for private and public clouds and probably more than one public cloud. The Cloud DBA is in the position to support this and provide statistics and details around these databases.

A catalog of the databases now includes application, database name, database platform, some basic baseline information, levels of high availability, cloud database, and location. The discovery along the way will continue to support these details and provide capacity information about the resources.

Workload and Data Analysis

The discovery is the baseline and the workload analysis provides the actuals to verify the forecasts. The workload is the size of the user data, and the number of transactions and processes. Sizes of backups of databases and movement from cloud to on-premise for any of these operations are included in the data analysis.

Examination of the workload should have details about the elasticity or constant activity of the processes. This is a critical question about handling workload and peaks for the cloud environment and how they plan to size it and provide additional resources.

The initial questions to evaluate the cloud platform should include these options, on-demand elasticity, data migrations from cloud to on-premise, and on-premise to cloud. These should be part of the cost evaluation to understand, depending on the workload and if the right platform is selected. This type of activity falls with the Cloud DBA because of the knowledge they possess about database environments, and they are probably already collecting these statistics and if not complete, they have the know-how to acquire it. Also important is the sensitivity for the data analysis for security.

The planning and estimates should provide the details to measure and compare the actuals. The discovery and workload analysis feeds the collection of the statistics to make it more predictable and prepare for future environments and growth.

Security

Security features of the cloud environment can then be configured to protect the data. The Cloud DBA is going to understand data protection and how to utilize the database features to prevent unauthorized access to the data. Security options are available but they need to be used and implemented.

In Oracle Cloud the databases come with the Oracle database security features. For example, encryption is enabled and tablespaces will need to be created using encrypt tablespace. The Cloud DBA needs to secure the database, the data at rest through encryption, and access controls using roles for authorizations. Auditing policies need to be enabled for auditing of the databases and monitoring of the activity.

The security options are part of the DBaaS Catalog and there are mandatory security features along with the options. Depending on the data compliance, regulations will apply. Installing the security components may not be necessary. However, implementing security will protect the data and the auditing will verify that the controls are in place.

Separation of Duties almost comes along with the fact that the database is in the cloud. The administration teams do not have access to the data, and the Cloud DBA does not have access to the server. It is now just dependent on making sure that data is isolated and protected through access controls and even using features such as an Oracle Database Vault to protect the data from highly privileged users. Security available on-demand with resources and databases seems to make it simpler for the Cloud DBA.

Migrations

This might actually be the first step in becoming a Cloud DBA, migrating to the cloud. Migrating to the cloud is a transforming process. It can be several systems at once or selectively choosing the databases for the types of cloud environments that they will best function in. As part of the transformation, the Cloud DBA can help along this journey.

The research should bring to the front details about cost savings, options for data access, and efficient mobile support. Cloud environments can provide an on-demand system that will allow the developers to work in and possibly bring the production environment back to a private cloud. This will highlight the business justification to move to the cloud and where it makes sense to be in a private cloud or stay on-premise.

The discovery pieces in capacity planning include looking at the baselines and reviewing the database sizing and analysis to determine which type of cloud infrastructure is going to support the migration. The questions also need to be asked to understand the roles the Cloud DBA is going to play.

Questions around maintenance schedules, workload capacity, and costs of data movement are a few to make note of to have answered before starting migrations. Understanding the responsibilities for the environment will prevent being able to restore or failover to DR. Main areas for understanding if it is the cloud provider or the Cloud DBA:

- Backups

- Patching

- High Availability

- Managing Failovers

- Managing Files and Backups

- Outage Reporting

The migrations do not stop once the database has moved over to the cloud. There are ongoing processes for a few reasons. There might be new data that will need to be migrated to the cloud. There might need to be a restore of a database on-premise to either perform tasks, test, or troubleshoot a problem. There are reasons to move data either for a new migration or in support of development environments. These types of data migrations need to be supported by the Cloud DBA. There should be a few different options to moving data such as cloning, attaching PDBs, and even Data Pump.

Migrations along with capacity planning can keep a Cloud DBA for quite awhile. Even though more databases are planned to be in the cloud, the future growth and movement of data between public, private, and on-premise is going to continue. It will help this migration to the Cloud help the on-demand environment grow.

Application vs. Cloud DBA

After examining all of the tasks of the Cloud DBA, there is similarity to a typical DBA. There are system tasks with backups and high availability, and there are object changes and data migrations. It is just different where the tasks are being accomplished. The installations are handled, configurations are in place with DBaaS options and deployments, but there is a need for understanding the databases and managing the activity in them. There are utilities that are used, but knowing to perform operations and looking to use automations when possible is the value of the Cloud DBA.

Transformation of the DBA to cloud is important for the databases in cloud to be successful for the applications. There is knowledge that the DBA possesses that provides the insight on tuning and capacity planning that is critical for the environment growth and performance. There are additional tasks that the Cloud DBA will perform that are not a complete match to the Application DBA, but since the database is using infrastructure in a private or public cloud the Cloud DBA does not have some of the tasks of the System DBA. Table 5-2 is a demonstration of some of the differences in tasks of the Application and Cloud DBA.

Table 5-2. *Cloud Service Models*

Tasks	Application DBA	Cloud DBA
Database Creation		X (DBaaS)
Patching		X
High Availability		X
Backups and Recovery	X	X
Data Migrations	X	X
Object Management	X	X
Access Controls	X	X
Encryption (Data Files)		X
Capacity Planning		X
Cloud Control Administration		X
Understanding Database Tools	X	X
Database Connections	X	X

Understanding that some of the tasks that are not checked as an Application DBA might actually be performed by some Application DBAs, and on the other side maybe the backups and recovery might not be performed. This is just an average number of DBA tasks to start to compare the importance of DBAs embracing the cloud environment and seeing what new opportunities are available.

Database creation does become self-service and on-demand, which means that application teams can also perform these tasks but then rely on the DBAs to help with maintenance, tuning, and future growth. Since the DBaaS service supplies the container and catalog for the databases, a DBA can be involved in creating the options and configurations that are in the DBaaS catalog.

DBaaS DBA vs. Cloud DBA

A DBA can work more on the development side and work with the containers. The DBA will need to understand what options and parameters can be configured and implemented as a standard across all of the databases. This will be the baseline of the DBaaS catalog. New features need to be researched by the DBA for compatibility with the DBaaS container. Having a DBA as part of the development team for DBaaS delivers a service that has the knowledge integrated into it for the best possible configuration. The basic database deployment will provide features that are needed and can be used by all. There can be different levels of support, security, or features that are in the catalog available to the applications.

The different levels are not selecting the specific parameters, it is selecting a service such as a high security option, warehouse database, or a level of performance. The grouping of options and parameters is the job of the DBA working on DBaaS. They develop the levels and know what belongs to those options. This also requires knowledge of the platform that the DBaaS databases are going to be deployed.

The Cloud DBA will use the DBaaS catalog and level choices in the catalog to create the databases in the cloud, and the DBaaS DBA will build the blocks and containers needed for the service. A DBaaS DBA will need to understand different programming languages, database development, and configurations. The DBaaS DBA will need to understand more of the infrastructure and the underlying cloud details with servers and OS to ensure that the containers will deploy properly in the cloud. The DBaaS DBA will test the containers and need to make sure that they can test the levels of services of the database. The validation of the database configurations and parameters can make sure that the databases are going to perform as expected and be turned over to the Cloud DBA for management.

Conclusion

A transformation to a Cloud DBA might be an easy path, and there are a few challenges as new tools need to be learned and become part of the day-to-day activities. Monitoring the databases for performance, security, and capacity is emphasized in the cloud. The options might be part of the options of the DBaaS and Cloud databases, but understanding the workings of the database will allow for the proper setup of the database in the cloud.

Migrations to the cloud create a whole new set of challenges, and the right questions need to be asked to make sure that responsibilities and services are clear so that the Cloud DBA can fill in the other activities and validate the other services and management of the cloud provider.

There are many databases that will be moving to public, private clouds, or both, and DBAs can be ready to support the migration and administration of the databases in cloud with the understanding of the roles and tasks that are utilizing the DBA's knowledge and skills.

CHAPTER 6

Database Security

Now we are at my favorite part of the book where I recruit you all to switch over to the security side. It is an area that you have to be passionate about because some days there is just one grant too many, but if you are a control freak and like solving puzzles, it is definitely something to consider. Wait, did I just call myself a control freak? Well, most DBAs are, but it is part of our superpowers, and we are just using them on the security side.

Security is everyone's responsibility, probably something you have heard before, but it is true. Protection of the company assets (data being the focus asset) is for everyone to participate in. The DBAs as the guardians of the data have a unique position and higher responsibility with the privileged access that has been entrusted to us. We have opportunities to drive security initiatives that reduce the risks in the database environments.

A DBA transformation to a security engineer or to the security is a logical step because of the skill sets both technical and soft skills. The database provides ways to secure the data and the DBAs know the day-to-day tasks that still need to be accomplished while also securing the privileged users.

Security Teams

Migrating over to a security team does not mean you have abandoned your DBA friends. It also does not mean that you can play a spy for the DBAs and continue to have possible risks in the environment. Moving to

© Michelle Malcher 2018
M. Malcher, *DBA Transformations*, https://doi.org/10.1007/978-1-4842-3243-9_6

the security team provides the working knowledge and technical skills to leverage the database to secure the systems and reduce risk across the enterprise.

Even though most of the security teams have been focused on network and protecting the perimeter, thoughts of not being able to get to the data have been considered. The database security to look specifically at protecting data assets is now something that security teams are looking to add and take the activity and audit logs from the databases to incorporate that into the overall security posture of the enterprise. The problem is a shortage of security engineers and qualified individuals to join the security teams, and plenty of people are needed because of the work and growth in this area.

Note   DBAs transforming to the security team bring a greater understanding of what jobs need to be accomplished while being able to secure the data.

Just watching the news and seeing the next data breach has convinced companies that they need to invest in security and make it a priority. That doesn't mean there are always resources, like people or time from other teams, but working on security allows the DBA to help prioritize the project and security work for the databases.

There is education that happens with security teams too. Depending on their backgrounds they might have different expectations of the database security, and clarification is going to allow the right security rules and policies to be put into place. There are even defaults that come with databases that should be discussed with the security team to take advantage of already existing security and look to what can be standardized across the enterprise.

Building a Team

There will be opportunities to build out database security teams. The team will work closely with the security teams to understand the auditing issues, policies, and priorities in the company for the security projects. The team will also work closely with the database teams as they will be part of the solution and project, whether they will be implementing it or observers of it. Remember the discussion of the soft skills that DBAs have naturally developed over the years, this is the perfect opportunity to utilize them. The collaboration between teams and communication will allow the DBA to transition to security and work on building a team of security engineers for implementation of database security.

The characteristics of a team are enterprise thinking, database skills, and willingness to continue to learn and research. Enterprise thinking is important because in large environments, manual processes are not going to be sustainable. The big picture is to include all of the possible database platforms and minimize solutions. Definitely not one solution fits all mentally, but how can a solution support and automate as much as possible to cover ground on many databases.

Teaching database experience is one way to develop this characteristic on the team, or teaching security is the other way to go. Most DBAs have been exposed to security just from the grants and roles that are created in the database. Also teaching an area that is not the main focus of the tasks might distract from the understanding of the database. Either way, a database security team member should have experience in one area and be able to learn in the other.

There are always new and not-so-new ways to use exploits and vulnerabilities. There are new tools that might make security easier. Just as with the database environments and how DBAs have constantly been learning the features and new releases, the security team is constantly researching and learning – good skills to have as a database professional, technology person, even just basically in life.

Security on DBA Team

Another option for database security is to take a couple of DBAs and just designate them with the security role. They would not shift over to the security team. This helps with some of the implementation of the security products and the DBAs with the security role can handle this effort. However, in being on the same team there might be a conflict of interest and the separation of duties might become blurred.

Staying as a DBA with just the focus of security can also make it difficult to just focus on security. Other priorities come up and other tasks might get in the way of the security. There are ways with roles to separate out Security DBAs from System and Application DBAs, so use of these roles will make it possible to only have the access needed. With these separations of duties for the DBAs, the reporting structure up to the database or security teams might not be as important.

Coordination with both the security and database is important. Knowledge and understanding of the database is important to have in order to effectively implement various security products and options. After team decisions are made and set up, the next step is to look at the security to be implemented and see how transforming from DBA will make sense.

Security Planning

Securing the database environment is a process. There are several configurations and products working together to provide the security. The planning needs to match up the enterprise security policies, compliance, and regulations with what is being implemented. Examples of standards can be found in the National Institute of Standards and Technology (NIST) Cyber Security Framework, if one set does not exist in your company. Even if one does, it might be worth evaluating it against the NIST cybersecurity framework.

Figure 6-1 stacks the different focus areas for these policies and what the security projects are going to fall under for implementation. They highlight the issues with the database environment that needs to have security wrapped around it for protecting the data.

Figure 6-1. *Main Areas where security is needed*

Authentication and authorization will handle password management and level of privileges. Ideally this would be a centralized repository for managing the users in the database. For Microsoft SQL Server, this would typically be Active Directory, and for Oracle either Oracle Unified Directory with Active Directory or other LDAP for users. The database user can be stored in one place and have security privileges managed with group access.

Data protection covers data at rest, in transit, and when accessed in the databases. Encryption of data at rest and in transit will protect the data files. Highly privileged users need to be handled differently to prevent unauthorized access to sensitive data. Activity monitoring sits on top of these configurations to confirm the proper controls and audit access and activity.

Regulations and compliance rules might be different for the location of the data or new rules might apply. It is a piece that security professionals need to understand the business, data, and requirements for the environment to comply to these regulations. For example, the General Data Protection Regulation (GDPR) will require any company with data from a citizen of the EU to comply with the regulation. The regulation needs to be reviewed and processes will need to be implemented to handle reporting a data breach within 72 hours of becoming aware. Notification is not the only process but the removal of the data from the system can also be requested. Security teams need to work with the database teams to get these processes and rules in place. Knowing the database like a DBA is definitely going to accelerate the ability to accomplish this.

Vulnerabilities and risk can be reduced with patching and maintaining the secure baselines. Patching has become easier for several database environments but still requires testing and managing of users' expectations of what maintenance windows and outages may occur. It is important to consider that the security fixes patch-known vulnerabilities so that reduces the risk in the environment.

Reducing Risk

Analyzing the risk in an environment helps to decide priorities and recognize the risks that are there. It allows for evaluation of the effort to reduce the risks and possible outcomes if it is not addressed. With all of the moving parts and how access is needed to the data, it is not likely that a database will be 100% secure, unless there was no access allowed to the server or database, and even then what if there was a backup that could be compromised.

The experienced DBA brings important understanding of the risks in the databases. There is knowledge about gap and if certain configurations are implemented how that protects or leaves other gaps in the environment. As DBAs are transforming to security, additional work is done focused on security to manage risk, where previous experience is focused on performance, resources, or other component of the database. This is a combination of the soft skills that are developed by the DBA to research the environment, create a plan, and communicate with various groups the discovered details and proposals of what to do about it.

For reducing risk, this is a high level of activities that are performed, including a loop back to review and test again.

- Understand the Risk

- Develop Mitigation Plan

- Report the Issue along with Mitigation Plan

- Evaluate Cost (Time/Money/Resources) to Mitigate

- Prioritize Efforts

- Review Risks Again

Security planning is based on this research of the risks in the environment and what has already been implemented to protect the data. Again, it is a continuous process to reduce risk in the database environment. Implementing security options, configurations, and products will work in preventing access to the data or performing malicious attacks on the environment.

Monitoring is a way to start to reduce risk and be able to know what is running and verify the configurations. The next step would be to be able to proactively handle the risk, and block malicious activity or unauthorized access from happening. This is a process to first understand which view into the environment helps to protect, then actually blocking and preventing for additional risk reductions. The process continues to monitor if there is any other activity that needs to be blocked. It almost sounds like a tuning process or troubleshooting, and it is very similar just focused on security.

The Security DBA will be able to identify risks, plan to mitigate the risks, prioritize, and communicate the risk and details of the remediation steps.

Cloud Security

We already discussed cloud database security in the previous chapter. However, as part of the security team, the scope is to incorporate the security plan of the cloud databases with policies to the overall security posture. The security offerings of the cloud need to be implemented and it is part of the security team to validate that the features are being used. The Cloud DBAs will be implementing the features and the Security DBA will be able to monitor and audit the security as seen in Figure 6-2. The cloud environment does simplify and reduce risk because of the automation and baselines that are implemented.

Figure 6-2. *Standardization Security in the Cloud*

Cloud database provide the baselines, and in a similar role the security professional can influence the options and levels of security that are needed in the cloud. These would be deployed consistently across the databases, which does simplify the auditing and validation of the security configuration.

Oracle database cloud will be providing databases that are autonomous and learning to handle malicious activity on the database. The computers are being trained to recognize this abnormal activity and can react faster than receiving an alert and especially read a very large report. The database can patch itself and apply the security fixes and not wait for a DBA to schedule a maintenance window, and they can still have the data available. This doesn't remove the need for database knowledge, as security and others are discussed in this book as opportunities to use these skills and gain new ones. Instead of having to worry about applying the patches, the focus can be other risks in the environment.

With databases in the cloud, security options should be researched, implemented, and validated. Options for the database in the different cloud providers can provide various levels of security. The Cloud DBA would be implementing the security options and the Security DBA will be reporting and verifying it.

Auditing and Reporting

Auditing can be accomplished in many ways, and the audit or reporting is only useful if it is being used. The security reports need to be reviewed for the abnormal activity and drift in configurations. Notifications and alerting would grab the attention of the security team to start drilling into any issue. These are all components of the monitoring and auditing from the security side. Policies are put into place for gathering details around highly privileged users and execution of certain activities. For many databases it is not something that can be accomplished manually, but it needs to be looked at analytically.

Security Information and Event Management (SIEM) tools can be used to gather these logs and analyze the data from the security logs for trends, which are behaviors to detect anomalies. DBA transformation to learn SIEM tools is a great possibility and leverages SIEM to report on the needed information and weed through the noise of a busy databases.

Configuration drift is part of the audit and checking because even if there are controls in place, there might be unauthorized access, a gap before the next level is implemented, or a new exploit being discovered. Auditing the configurations and baselines will be needed for the audits and provide opportunities to address the issues and understand what else might be happening. The security team can also be updating baselines as new features are implemented or change in versions or platform of the database require new standards.

Audit policies also need to be implemented and researched by the security team. They can make sure that as databases and applications change, the right information is being captured. There might be other information that flows through the SIEM tool that is gathered to provide even better policies and other details. Audit policies are based on the enterprise policies and what is being met in the security tool implementations. Checks and validations can be set up to automatically check and report on.

Automation Security

Individual policies and databases are not going to each be examined by the security team. They need tools and automation to make this happen. Just as with the new offerings from cloud databases, the trend is for the database and technology to handle the work. Self-driving databases are what Oracle is talking about. This gives us the answers and information, but policies and some of the actions need to be determined by the Security

DBA. It can let the database patch for remediation of known issues but processes need to be developed for automation and included to match up processes and checks.

With the amount of security and audit logging, automation of reviewing to provide alerts or proactive changes needs to be part of the database environment for security.

Addressing Vulnerabilities

Addressing vulnerabilities is not just about patching, ok mostly about patching but it does require some additional information. As risk is being reduced in an environment through other security measures, it might not be as easy to exploit. The pieces and controls in the environment need to be included in the assessment. Even with database applying its own patches and reducing risk, vulnerabilities that are outside of the software or built into other application code need to be examined.

DBAs are use to testing and working through upgrades and after patching and patch sets are applied. Security fixes might be part of the first set of fixes, but additional areas might be covered as part of a bigger patch set.

Security teams need to take into consideration the various tools, monitoring, auditing, and blocking that is configured to provide weighted details about the risk. Weighted scores for vulnerabilities are part of the Common Vulnerability Scoring System (CVSS) and is from National Vulnerability Database. The list of vulnerabilities and scores are reported here with details about the vulnerability. This information along with any vendor information can be used to assess the risk in the current environment.

The vulnerabilities are another reason that database knowledge on the security team is important, as details of how it can be exploited might not mention much information, but a DBA might understand it more and realize that it is a higher or lower risk then scored.

Security Learning

DBAs enjoy that they are always learning. There are new databases platforms, cloud environments, and new security risks and vulnerabilities. The security teams also have to continue to learn and research the details of possible exploits and research issues that might have happened. There are tools that are being used and with AI, the databases and machines are also learning.

Learning is not just one sided with the security teams. Education has to be passed along to others. The database options are not going to fill in all of the gaps, so education is around what layers of security are handling the different risks.

Instruction around access and process helps to explain how they should be participating in the security in the environment. DBAs are focused on the development or systems of high availability to get their tasks done. They are not focused on the security and even though they may be concerned about the access, they might not know or understand the tools that they have to implement the security.

As the security team, design, process, and documentation need to be created to provide to the DBAs and others using the database to include them in the processes. These will keep the environments consistent and using the same secure configurations. Information around auditing will also help to keep them honest with the procedures and processes as well as protect them from activity that might occur.

Providing new information and project planning for overall enterprise security needs education for the various teams. DBAs will be interested to know the perimeter security around their databases and the other teams will receive information on how the data is being protected. Allow the teams to understand the security requirements and become part of the projects and solutions to support the security initiatives for the databases in the future too.

The Security DBA needs to be able to explain to management about the potential risks and help them to comprehend the priorities of the risk remediation. It is not the same as putting permissions on a file for read, write access. The granularity of the database security is much deeper. The solutions and risk mitigation for the solutions are going to be more complex and detailed. The databases also affect other applications and how they behave so the layers of applications to database must be taken into consideration with the security of the system. Explanations and education up and down the company ladder are requirements for any security professional to help inform and help in making decisions for what comes next.

The Security Professional is going to be securing the database environment. There are serious concerns about the vulnerabilities, issues, and other risks associated with database access and unauthorized access from internal and external sources. Figure 6-3 shows the security solution stack to start with in applying encryption, privilege management especially for privileged users, least privilege roles and groups, monitoring and auditing, and patching that will help protect against vulnerabilities.

Figure 6-3. *Security Solutions for the Database*

Conclusion

In the cloud or on-premise the database security is a responsibility of a team. The security team can support the enterprise policies and baselines in the database. It is the knowledge of the database that makes it easier to know where the risks are and prioritize the initiatives. The DBA that is transitioning to the security role has the opportunity to learn skills for managing the security and audit logs in SIEM tools. DBAs can utilize their skill set in order to design how to mitigate vulnerabilities and risk in the environment. With automation processes, the monitoring analysis becomes preventative actions to protect the data.

CHAPTER 7

Data Professionals

It is all about the data. There is value in the data and as more information becomes available through mobile and IOT devices, our imaginations start to bring us ideas of the potential of what can be realized with the right data.

Just like inventions, there are reasons and purpose for needing something that triggers ideas of what can be developed. Several areas of data already follow these innovations. Sports, retail, health care, manufacturing, marketing, and plenty of other industries see data as a company asset. The enterprise realizes the importance of data and has many data sources, but it needs the direction of what to do with this information. Analyzing the data and providing questions to ask is the competitive edge in using the data.

Over the past few years the office of the Chief Data Officer (CDO) has developed to become an integral part of more enterprises. The role is to manage and provide governance for the highly valuable data assets of the company. The data that flows through the company and realizing that there is more information to gather requires a team of individuals strictly focused on the business needs for data and architecting where data is available and ensuring the quality of the data.

DBAs that have been working on data services and other data workflows can find ways to transform into the data professional. They can provide guidance on how the data is captured, used, and distributed to other applications and provide the know-how of the database processes to efficiently work with the data.

© Michelle Malcher 2018
M. Malcher, *DBA Transformations*, https://doi.org/10.1007/978-1-4842-3243-9_7

Data Quality

Data coming in through different sources will have to go through data quality processes. There are controls and tagging of the data to ensure that it is accurate, classified, and complete. Companies will have various types of data all needing governance on how it can be used and what needs to be secured. Also available are external data sources that can fill in gaps and additional attributes to provide a complete data set to be used.

Master Data Management (MDM) is generally what is considered as the overall work for data quality. MDM can be part of any system that pulls data through work processes and offers data services as the system of record or the golden data set. There needs to be a catalog that will provide details about the data classification and how it should be used and the source of the data. DBAs are supporting these processes and management of data in the databases. They have the insight to improve data processing and where data is available to include additional attributes.

Data models and flow will be known to help them transform into more of a data profession to plan, develop, and integrate processes to support MDM and especially data quality. Data quality is an interesting process and is continuous because new data is always coming and new sources are made available. The quality follows a development process. The following is how to look at that process:

- Gather requirements for the needed data

- Gather information about the sources

- Write procedures to bring in data

- Write procedures to fill in the required attributes and gaps

- Write procedures to validate the data (remove duplicates, incomplete data)

- Capture data issues

- Write processes to address data issues

- Perform cleansing processes

- Validate against data requirements

This list includes the writing of procedures and running through the process that is the testing and development of the data quality workflow. After being tested, validated, and deployed, the procedures would run automatically. Some of the data issues might require manual intervention to figure out what the issue is, but then they can be included in the cleansing process. The business requirements can change, which will mean that the procedures and cleansing processes will need to be modified.

MDM is not a simple decision and requires efforts from everyone involved in the data sources and use of the data. These projects are developed based on sources of data needed and business questions and processes to get the needed information in the right hands to execute upon them.

Tip   MDM is not just the job of the DBA, and it is difficult to do data cleansing if other processes are not on board with the quality of the data. Business requirement, development effort, and data professionals along with the business need to work together to support MDM.

Working on these processes, developing code to be executed as part of data quality is part of a database developer type role and is a transition for a DBA to focus specially on these areas. The database system is going to require less hands-on maintenance and administration, which opens up this opportunity to look at data processes. Providing data source and services is going to be critical for the enterprises' business processes and understanding the available data is going to lead to better questions. Better questions about the data will lead to new opportunities and hopefully provide a competitive edge with customers and other business partners.

Data quality and governance also supplies analytics and analysis of the data. Analytics are performed on many data sets to get answers to questions. There are plenty of uses for this in companies, but as an example, think of your spending habits and location details being collected for credit card suppliers to detect potential misuse of credit cards and identity theft issues.

Having sources that are not the golden source of data or uncleansed data is not going to produce accurate analytics or analysis of the data. If there are gaps in the location of the use of the credit card that might not be able to supply that, the card is being used in two different places and it could be fraud or other issues with the credit card account. Early detection of this and details will depend on how fast the data can move through the analysis process that the data is going through; this is a logical place for a DBA to step in to help with performance and even look how the analytics are performing on the processes. The knowledge of the DBA can cleanse and transform the data that is part of the analytics.

Data quality frameworks are available to work from that to match up the data quality steps with business requirements. Figure 7-1 shows the process of going through a framework for data quality.

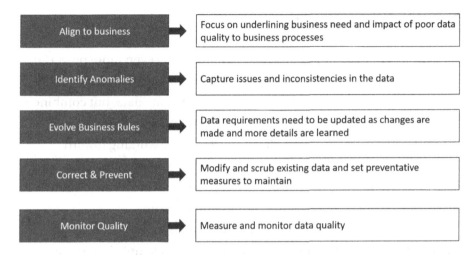

Figure 7-1. *Data Quality Steps*

Classification of the data will also contain data that needs specific keys about personal and sensitive data. Classifying data will allow other security and business processes to utilize that knowledge about the data to make sure that it is properly secured and only made available to authorized uses.

The CDO office and teams work to handle MDM and the data quality processes. They work with the business to understand what data sources are needed and the business requirements for data analytics. They take the sources of the data and provide the governance and workflows. The classification of the data is not just important for the business but extremely beneficial for technology processes. This can provide additional information about the data source and if it is the source of record and information about security. Security tools can use classification of the data for monitoring and access controls.

Data Integrations

The data sources do not just sit alone. They become even more powerful when they work together. There are enough challenges with data quality and understanding the details about the source of the data, but combine that with data coming from different platforms and with different descriptions of the data. Hopefully the CDO will be working toward standardizing the details around the data details and classifications, so the only challenge is to be able to combine the data into a single source without losing data changes from the system of record.

DBAs have opportunity here to maintain data sources, how to integrate the data and design processes to allow for simple integrations to other sources. Data integration tools are available to catalog the business rules and keep the definitions of the integration process. It has ways to implement data quality procedures and keep a system of record information. The DBA transformation can be with learning new tools such as Oracle Data Integrator (ODI). ODI is a tool specifically to create the process and procedures for the data integrations. It is an ongoing process and there are consistently new data that is required by the business or used to enhance current sources. These tools are additional to the database tools, but with the understanding of database objects, they are something that DBAs can master.

Not all of the data sources are going to be in databases. There are going to be different forms of data, such as APIs or files. There might be extract, load, transform (ETL) processes needed to use the source. Then there is being able to use the data in sources closest to the golden copy to prevent duplication and synchronization issues.

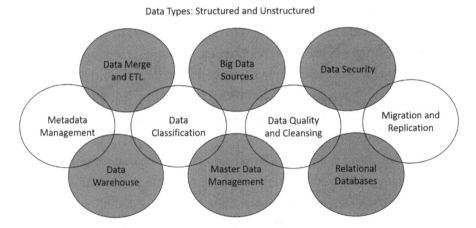

Figure 7-2. *Data Integration Data and Processes*

Figure 7-2 is a way to look at processes and data sources that can make up the data integrations. There is quite a bit of effort for designing a robust integration for the data, because it takes in all of these details just discussed in data quality, conversations with the business to understand the data strategies, and exploring the sources of different data sources available.

Data professionals are going to work with data integration tools, test data quality, maintain business rules, and continue to review the rules and data sources. The processes of ETL and producing APIs are going to be constantly monitored and challenges come with real-time data and speed of which the data is needed for the business.

BIG DATA

Big Data is not about large amounts of data. It is about data coming in structured or non-structured form with high velocity. Big Data is going to use other technology platforms such as Hadoop, NoSQL, and Massively Parallel Processing (MPP) databases. The data collection can be coming in from sources such as IOT devices, social media, and even several public sources of data sets.

DBAs can currently be pulling in big data sources into the relational databases to provide full data sources in other systems. The opportunities here for the DBA are to learn the Big Data technologies. Hadoop is a platform that can process the data coming in from devices and other data sets. It is not necessarily the administration of the technologies or platforms, but how to use them and use the data sets to integrate with other database systems.

As we look into a data professional, you can notice that these processes start with data quality, and then proceeds to data integrations and repeat data quality. Each step along the way might be looking at data quality. The velocity and amount of data that comes in with the Big Data sources challenges these processes to see if data quality matters or if certain pieces of the data is what is important. The data might be used for analytics in a way that just the processes need to run and not all require the complete data set. There are several details to consider when looking at these data sets and are they available to augment the existing data that is collected through another Big Data process or the relational data. Also think about the security that is needed for data. If it is public information, it might not need the security processes in place until it is integrated with other data. This integration might become the company's intellectually property.

Business intelligence is based on all of the data points that are coming in from Big Data sources, other data integrations, and then the algorithms can help provide the data science around the details. The questions are part of the business intelligence to answer the right questions and provide answers or start to provide direction to make decisions.

Data professionals are managing the Big Data processes, using the new tools that come with it. Understanding how to use Hadoop, analytical processes, and other NoSQL databases are going to be key for this area. The public data sources with data that is collected is going to be available to use as part of the business strategies for data and integrations.

Conclusion

DBAs have the knowledge of where data is available or have at least an idea when data moves. It is normally a process that they have been involved in from the beginning. Even if it was not to know what the data is being used for, it could be to improve the speed of the process or help make the appropriate connections or load data into the database.

These interactions with the data are a foundation for moving more into the data field. However, most of the movement, migrations, and loading of the data should become automated processes. The databases still house the information and being able to catalog the data and provide the details about the metadata builds the components of what the data is about and how it can be used.

The teams under the CDO are looking for that knowledge and understanding about how to use, move, and integrate data to meet business needs. The data is a valuable company asset that can be underutilized if the knowledge is not there on how to use it or what questions it can answer.

Information is captured at a single point in time; these are our data records. This will get fed into a system to be able to gather details around all of this information and provide knowledge and analysis about the data of what it means, how it applies to the business, and what can be learned by it. This is the knowledge that is trying to be understood and comprehended by the applications to translate what that means to business processes. As data points change over time, they are captured and provides combined sets of data for decision making and business intelligence.

The collection of the data and applying the business rules give us the insight into the data. They knowledge of the data is based over time and collection of the information. As the sources are explored and how they should be utilized are part of the knowledge of the data, and the processes and workflows provide the other pieces for understanding the sources. It is the applications and business processes that make it possible to have the knowledge about what the data is telling us and how it applies to the business and even technology processes.

DBAs have the opportunity to work even closer with the data. Data quality and integrations are part of the data processes that are run to provide accurate and complete data to answer questions and provide business knowledge back to the business. These data sources and understanding how to manage and utilize them are what data professionals do. The DBA transformation comes with wanting to support the business strategies with the business intelligence provided by efficient, standardized, and accurate data processes. The data professional will perform these tasks to cleanse and attach to the data source to the correct workflows. Automation of the processes will not be removing the need for DBAs or Data Professionals because the knowledge and understanding of the data flows still needs to be mapped and processes is part of that education to become a data professional.

CHAPTER 8

The Art of Automation

DBAs learn that if they have to perform a task twice, it is worth the time and effort to automate it. There are scripts, and multiple scripts are part of the DBA arsenal. It feels that there is not always the time to automate because there is a way to quickly execute a script and pass along a script for further management. However, in the environments that we will be dealing with, automation is essential. There are too many databases, and the more tasks and times they are executed, it allows for the possibility of an error of a manual action to occur.

Automation prevents tasks from being skipped and be logged along with the script changes going through change control. Automation is an art of recognizing patterns that should not require hands-on keyboard and a state that is desired. Just as with security, data quality, and other processes, this is an iterative cycle. The tasks can be automated, and then new tasks and other processes that were not first considered can be added to the list. It can start with the initial database tasks, look to other components such as security, data migrations, and reach out to application with an additional circle of automation, including the environment tasks.

The art of automation requires reviewing older processes that might have been automated already and verify that they are still a valid way of doing things. The DBA scripts several processes with previous versions of the database, and the new features need to be updated in the scripts. The possibility of automating updates would be interesting but might not be possible. The circle of automation might start with some administration tasks and then continue to incorporate more and more. The attempt to

M. Malcher, *DBA Transformations*, https://doi.org/10.1007/978-1-4842-3243-9_8

automate everything might make sense, but there might be difficulties with some jobs, and review with new releases of the tools and databases to leverage to implement the automations.

DBA transformation understands the patterns of the tasks and workflows to be able to instruct which jobs and tasks should be automated. Even once jobs are automated, there are other opportunities to include new tasks or review any gaps or processes that should be considered. The application processes can then be included as well as other processes of the environment.

Tasks

There are many areas of the databases that can be automated. On the operations side, jobs like backups, patching, storage, and high availability tasks can have automated processes in place. Other options might be to look for tuning and security automations. Automating tasks is ongoing and it is not to take away from the positions of the DBAs but free up opportunities to perform other jobs in working on projects and reviewing various details of the databases such as new features.

Table 8-1 has a list of tasks that seem to be manual or might be something that is still being run manually because of resource constraints.

Table 8-1. *Manual Tasks to review*

Tasks	Execution	Validation	Success/Failure
Backups	Scheduled	Available in OEM and log files	Reports with complete or errors for failures
Adjusting resource capacity	Manual add storage, auto adjust memory	Additional space added	Additional space available or errors reported
Patching	Executing the patching script with pre- or post-tasks	Available log	Reports with success or failure with error messages
Standby Failover	Manual failover to standby database with data guard manager	Running on failover node	Logging into standby as primary, use data guard manager to validate the status of the primary and standby databases
Tuning	Manual capture of SQL statements for tuning	Statements Captured	Benchmarks for performance improvements
Security Audit Reports	Run reports for auditing	Review of reports	Captured data for audits
Refresh of development data	Manually run jobs to refresh	Test database refreshed	Access to test database successful

The tasks listed in Table 8-1 are just a sample of the various jobs that can be automated either through scripts that can be scheduled or part of a process that gets executed and passes criteria to the next job for execution.

Dependencies

Automations can come with dependencies in the system: either a task that must run first or a piece of data that is needed. An action can trigger another action and a piece of data that is needed can trigger another action. This is sometimes why automations might not be put in place because of complexities of the systems or steps that have to be followed. I will argue that it is for this reason that jobs like this need to be automated. Anytime that there is a dependency and a task requires a pre- or post-step these should be sequenced automated jobs.

The database provides DBMS_SCHEDULER and can handle multiple steps and passing in of values to the different processes in the job. Other scheduler software will also take this into consideration when executing the automated processes. There are many tasks that need to be run on the application and database side that need to support to validate execution and dependencies in the jobs.

The DBA transitioning to do automations has opportunities to script out processes, do database development, examine processes for migration to automation, and conduct testing with regular testing plans and QA.

Automating Test Plans

Database and software development require structured testing and QA. The database environments need to be refreshed to handle this too. As part of the database automation, the unit testing tools can be used and automated tests can be developed for the database testing. Application code is normally set up for the automation, but the database scripts of tables, data changes, etc., will work in the unit testing using something like SQLDeveloper. These tests can verify database objects and upgrade of objects.

Having the test plans automated makes it easier to test database changes, upgrades, and other processes on the database. There are other tools to use besides SQLDeveloper and there is also Real Application Testing (RAT), and this captures workload with a way to regression test it. The unit testing is providing testing opportunities with Agile developers to test the code and database objects as part of an automation plan.

Figure 8-1 shows the place to get started with the SQLDeveloper tool for Unit testing.

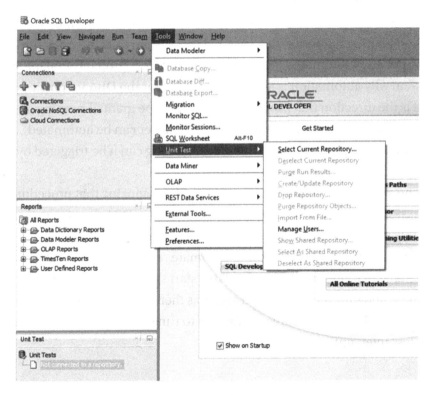

Figure 8-1. *Unit testing in SQLDeveloper*

Automation processes and unit testing make it possible for DBAs to transition to discovering, maintaining, and creating automated processes around these database jobs and testing procedures.

Conclusion

With the Autonomous Database recently announced, the role of the DBA is definitely changing. Then it seems like more processes are automatically being configured. The database is able to deliver more automation on its own and provide configurations already implemented and even backups in place. The self-driving database is available in Oracle Cloud and it automates the management and performance tuning of the database.

The database automation of the Autonomous Database is based on machine learning and provides stability and performance because of the few human interactions of these needed tasks. From a security perspective, it also provides automated patching. This example is probably making you question why automation is another possibility for the DBA in transition, but it is the direction that processes have to go. The manual running of processes is definitely a thing of the past. Whatever can be automated should be, and if you can't automation something can it be triggered by one that can.

The art is to understand the patterns and recognizing that procedures and tasks should be automated for the databases. A DBA transformation into this area is more coding and becoming a manager for the development processes and how to automate refreshes and unit testing for database components. The processes start specifically around the database and may then expand in scope as there are ways to look at how we work, and there are more possibilities to run code more efficiently and with less intervention.

CHAPTER 9

Change and Cloud Therapy

Database Administrators enjoy working with databases. They are challenging environments that, if supported properly, provide extreme value to the company. To be able to support many applications, different industries, and several departments within the enterprise exposes a DBA to many facets of the company. This is what gives a DBA satisfaction with their job. They understand the value they bring to many areas and are able to continue to contribute by providing a highly available and well-performing database.

Note *USA Today*'s list of the "Ten Happiest Jobs in America" from spring 2015 stated that the Oracle DBA is sixth on the list for being the most happy.

Technology jobs are in demand but the skills tend to shift. This shift or disruption that we have been talking about is cloud. Of course there are others with big data with IOT devices and security. As discussed in previous chapters, with cloud services, there is significant growth in migrations to the cloud. There is also a need to understand data problems and protect the data.

© Michelle Malcher 2018
M. Malcher, *DBA Transformations*, https://doi.org/10.1007/978-1-4842-3243-9_9

We are not just DBAs! There is an incredible amount of knowledge gathered over the years from development, and from the business and other teams that you have worked with over the years. Being able to plan different projects for upgrades, data security, and migrations – just to name a few – demonstrate part of the soft skills developed over the years as well.

DBAs are used to change and the journey to the cloud or other DBAs' transformation should be part of the job. Not having consistent days and plenty of work to do are the challenges that are enjoyed. So why is there resistance to change how we work? We are comfortable with changes in our normal environment, but it is time to look at the journey.

Job Satisfaction

Knowing that data is such a valuable part of the enterprise, being able to provide a service is the sense of job satisfaction. A successful day might be being able to answer questions, solve some troubleshooting problems, and knowing that you have been adding value to the company.

Think about what it is you enjoy about being a DBA.

- No day is the same

- Performance tuning

- Upgrades

- Managing users and objects

- Working with other teams

- Designing the data model

- Automating processes

- Solving data questions

- Implementing new features

- Providing a service

- Hardware administration

- Storage maintenance

- Migrations

- Consolidations

I am sure you can think of plenty of other reasons or combination of reasons to find enjoyment in the job. It is important to find something that is interesting, fun, and enjoyable about the job. It might be the technology, people, or even the tasks.

Challenges are needed because it keeps us learning and growing. The experiences that we collect get us ready for the next challenge. We have already discussed the next challenges in previous chapters so now we just have to figure out where you fit in with that.

Just because things are changing is not a reason to be concerned. In the world of databases, things are always changing, and this time we have some pretty big technology disrupters that we are dealing with in the cloud, security, and what about autonomous databases.

The cloud is a satisfying place too. There are strategies for data to develop and be secure in cloud environments. These challenges and new environments should energize and excite a DBA for opportunities in a shift in job tasks.

Cloud Therapy

The cloud is everywhere. There are database, software, security, OS, and so many other services in the cloud. We need to look at these services as ways to enhance the environment; or if we are doing private cloud, what other cloud services we should be providing in our private clouds.

The cloud environments tend to give us hesitation because of some unknowns. Remember back in Chapter 2 when we discussed the control factor: the DBAs need to be able to control pieces of the environment in order to make sure it is configured as needed. But the cloud has some unknowns and may not always appear to have the same support as if it was offered by you. However, the DBA can most definitely verify settings and configurations to make sure that they are meeting service-level agreements.

It is this understanding of what the environments should be provided that helps to verify and feel comfortable with the cloud system that we can work with. The databases are not changing but how we are supporting them is.

Concerns with migrating to the cloud have been covered in several of the previous chapters. According to the IOUG Database Cloud Survey, 2016, the top five concerns are the following:

- Security and Privacy

- Data Ownership and Retention

- Software Licensing Issues

- Lack of Expertise or Knowledge

- Regulatory Compliance

These are areas for development with the DBA and as we have these topics clarified for our enterprise, they will support the changes in the environment. Data ownership seems to be issues that we even face now. This will continue to be important with data as a service and will need to be tagged for the business and application as the data owner.

As competition between the cloud providers continues, it is possible that licensing will be not be a concern. But there still needs to be expertise of the cloud environment along with questions and validations for compliance. The DBAs can address these concerns in the environment with what they know.

If you think about the hardest part of on-premise deployments, the server and storage procurement takes time and may not be as elastic. IT resources need to be available for deploying and configuring servers.

Questions that need to be asked of cloud providers to ensure proper services are the following:

- What are the options and parameters that are used?

- How do they store sensitive data?

- Cloud types offered and how to migrate?

- What are the maintenance options?

- How do large data sets migrate or load into the cloud?

- What are the costs? Look at transactions or load. Is there on-demand usage?

This is a quick list and not all inclusive of questions to ask.

Even if we are thinking the cloud environment is not something the industry or company you work for might be using, there are reasons to migrate. There are development environments or other applications that would benefit from the use of the cloud. It is important to understand and advise which databases will perform well in the cloud. This is also the opportunity to embrace cloud environments and help direct the migrations of what type of clouds can be used.

From database as a service to cloud, it does change how we work or where we work, but it helps to direct and recommend the best environment. To be able to be part of the solution is going to make for an easier transition. Resisting that the cloud environment is coming or something to migrate to will just make it more difficult to stay involved with the new cloud.

Change Management

Change by leading is what is going to allow for greater involvement in the future direction. It will embrace the differences in how work is accomplished or where it is performed. The enterprise is working to be more efficient and saving operational costs as these changes are put into place. Again we have options to embrace change or stay the same.

Change is not easy. We do get comfortable in our positions and tasks, and knowing what is expected. Even learning new features and making changes to new versions of the database is not as much of a change but is easier than how we have to work or changing what we do. This is also something that we enjoy about the job in the first place: that things change in the environment. Of course it does not always change our perspective or how we have to work, which is different now with this migration to the cloud. The different types of DBAs can examine their favorite pieces of the job and look to invest in additional learning to make that change and continue to add value to the company.

Leading Change, a book by John P. Kotter (Harvard Business Review Press, 2012), discusses the process of making these major changes.

- Changing a career or leading change in your company can follow these steps to be successful in dealing with the change and helping others, such as your team members, to make the change with you.

- Establishing a sense of urgency, and with the statistics about the movement to the cloud and technology direction, the time is now.

- Creating a group to work together with enough influence to lead the change.

- A vision and strategy needs to be developed so that the goal is recognized and understood.

- Part of understanding is communicating the change vision, including modeling the behavior that is needed to embrace this change.

- Empowering broad-based action, and getting rid of the obstacles.

- Generate short-term wins, and this will make the change visible quicker than the long-term projects.

- Consolidate gains that produce more change. Effect changes increases the credibility to change all systems, structures, and policies.

- Anchor new approaches in the culture, which provides the connection to the new behaviors and successful changes.

The vision and strategy will have everyone on the same page and a common goal. It takes more than one DBA to move to the cloud and perform migrations. There should also be discussions around what each of the team members can do that will empower them and provide a sense of responsibility with a new environment and possibly a new role.

Change is needed to keep the company competitive. Change is needed as we look to keep current in our skills and be involved in technology. Embrace the disruption and enjoy the change and opportunities it brings. Encourage team members and look for those quick acceptance changes that will keep everything moving forward.

Work–Life Balance

Working as a technologist has definitely provided ways to work from anywhere and also have flexible hours. Because of all of the individual tasks that have to be completed and lack of automation, there have been many days and nights that the DBA has spent on the phone and working with support issues. This is something that most of the DBAs should be celebrating as we look to migrate to service-oriented architecture and cloud. With changes in how to support the data and automation, there is a possibility for more time to enjoy life outside of the office instead of on support calls. The time and availability might even allow you to think about sharing your migration experiences with user communities and volunteer for a group like Independent Oracle User Group (IOUG).

Along with time to volunteer, the regular workday leaves us with time to work on the projects and research the areas we have for our environments. The automation of processes gives us the chance to do this and focus on business needs and not just individual task execution.

Of course work–life balance means different things to different people, but we still all need opportunities to recharge. It is easy to get exhausted if we are dealing with the same issues and need a change. This might be a good opportunity to look into ways to unplug, recharge, and enjoy reading your favorite technology book.

We tend to be passionate about what we do, and our jobs become our hobby. It does not help when we are looking at work–life balance. However, we do need to prioritize the work that we do and make sure that we have other opportunities to develop skills and continue to learn.

Skill Development

Recognizing that change and the cloud environment are going to be the current future direction, along with planning migrations, includes skill development. It probably is something already in the works. Understanding these new environments and what skills are of interest to you can be developed as part of the migration plan.

Skill development comes from doing and through training. On of the best parts about the cloud environment is that it is available for testing and learning. Oracle Cloud even provides discounts to get into the environment, test, and start to verify configurations. The cloud is a perfect training ground as it is easy to set up and get running.

Test Environments

The cloud can be a test environment for looking at migrations or upgrades. These are the systems to build up skills and look at ways to help any projects move forward with testing. The operational expenses are reduced along with the cost of additional hardware when we are able to utilize the cloud.

Applications can also test upgrades and it can be a sandbox for new releases. How many times are new test environments requested and needing to be maintained? This can be one of the automated processes even for a development on-demand database. Oracle can even clone pluggable databases from on-premise databases.

Many frameworks are available in the cloud, so they can all be part of the testing to simulate workloads and test new features. These types of automated, on-demand test environments support the Agile development processes and provide environments for DBAs to test features that normally are difficult to test in other databases.

Life Learner

Wanting to develop new skills and being in the database, it is almost a given that you are a lifetime learner. This keeps skills up to date. The skills we learn are for the new technologies encountered as we see opportunities to enhance our environments.

To be a life learner, it requires self-motivation, excitement, and passion about the technologies and areas of focus. However, sometimes we have to learn about areas maybe like cloud or a server service that might not be as interesting as our ultimate goals. As you are doing this, without learning about areas that you are not sure about, you end up learning even more and verify that your passion is in the right place.

Conclusion

The cloud and change require DBAs to consider the concerns and opportunities of these environments. It definitely is not an easy task to lead change and move from our comfort zone to new roles and tasks. Reviewing tasks that are enjoyed help to know what needs to be learned and provide us comfort that not everything is changing.

CHAPTER 10

Creating a Transformation Plan

We realize we have to make a change. The cloud environment and databases as a service is the next stage that is to be faced and planned on until the next disruption. With the skill sets that are gathered by DBAs, there are plenty of opportunities. With the databases in the cloud and Oracle Autonomous databases, there are processes that no long require a DBA, but the database understanding is important for the enterprise. DBAs need to transform into a couple of different roles to provide this expertise. We have a choice, and that is a great thing it means that you can choose a direction that fits with the areas you like to do. I did this a few years back in choosing security.

Security has always been an area that I have been interested in, and in working with different security products, I preferred setting up the security options and managing those. So it made sense when given the opportunity to go to the security team and handle the database security projects; it was a perfect fit. The fun part is I get to continue to learn new security skills, keep database knowledge, and work with several different teams for planning and implementing.

© Michelle Malcher 2018
M. Malcher, *DBA Transformations*, https://doi.org/10.1007/978-1-4842-3243-9_10

Tip   Decide on the skills that give you the most satisfaction in your job. There are going to be new opportunities in that area and new skills to learn too.

This is an opportunity to review the database environment, assess your skills, and put together a transformation plan.

Transformation

Throughout the chapters, we discussed the options for transformation. The work as a DBA develops many technical and soft skills. Now it is time to review this DBA Toolbelt and consider what the next steps are in this process. Figure 10-1 demonstrates that all of these endpoints start with the DBA skills and the evaluation that is now needed to get to the next stage.

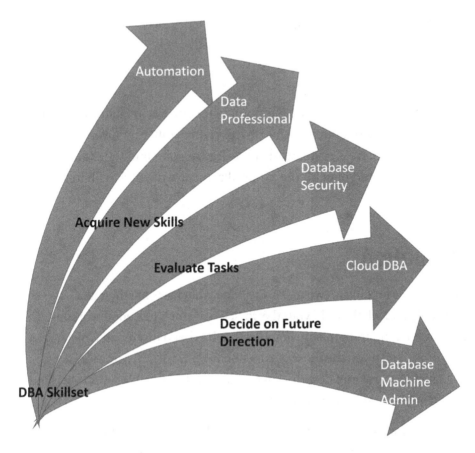

Figure 10-1.   *Transformation from DBA skills*

The DMA, Cloud DBA, Security, Data Professional, and Automation Engineer are only five paths that you can take or a combination of these. There are other paths that are available; some might be less technical and more people oriented, for example, management roles to help prepare teams to manage the cloud. There might also be even more technical roles with development or systems. These three steps will gather the details that are needed for the transformation.

- Decide on the Future Direction

- Evaluate Tasks

- Acquire New Skills

The future direction is the endpoint of the arrows in Figure 10-1. It is also possible to work through this process with a different future direction that is not listed. Next evaluate the tasks for the roles and the skills that are your strengths, and plan for the new skills that are needed to fill in the gaps for the role.

Evaluation

Evaluation is looking at two areas. Evaluate what tasks are the most enjoyable and what would your day look like if you had a good workday. This is to understand from the previous list that has been discussed which areas are going to give you the most satisfaction from work and career choices.

This is a very brief description for each of the possible DBA roles, and the chapters on each can be used for more details as evaluating.

- **Database Machine Admin (DMA)** – System DBA like but needs to administer storage cells and OS

- **Cloud DBA** – Application DBA like, limited access to the server, additional monitoring responsibilities because of the cloud environment

- **Database Security** – Security tools, auditing, access controls, and work with security and data teams

- **Data Professional** – Big Data, Business Intelligence, data quality, and integrations

- **Automation** – Writing and developing automation processes, monitoring jobs

These new roles can enhance your career, which will still provide support for the company's data assets. The disruptors are rapidly changing the environment that we have been working in and the evaluation will help sort out which role fits them best without having to fear the direction of the new environment. After evaluating which new roles are ideal for you, it is time to look at current and needed skills.

New Skills

Compare the DBA's base skill set with the other roles' additional learning and development for different roles. The database skills are the commodity that the company wants to keep when migrations happen to the cloud environments. The DBAs should view this as an opportunity for that very reason.

What happens when we don't develop new skills? That is when we need to have fear about the changes that are coming to the databases. The work and effort that we do can be redirected to other areas very quickly, and a company is looking to reduce costs by consolidation of servers or utilize an elastic service for the databases with the cloud. They are looking to keep the experience and support the knowledge of the data, integrations, and the business intelligence.

Planning

Not all DBAs will have the same experiences. Others might have had more time working with high availability and others working with teams building communication and relationships. These are both the technical and soft skills that are needed, but one DBA might have gaps just because of the difference in the environment and company.

Figure 10-2 demonstrates a quick sheet for helping to gather that detail around the skills and understanding the gaps that would be the ones that still need to be learned. The circles represent a continuous process. Just as we are facing a shift in technology and the databases automation, there will be more coming in the future, and this is not the last time.

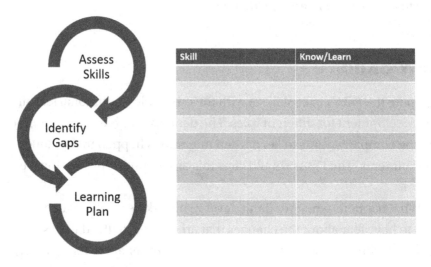

Figure 10-2. *Skill Learning Plan*

The gaps might even be for strengthening skills. DBAs have communication, leadership, and organizational skills, but there might need to be courses in leadership or reviewing process skills to enhance what is already there.

Database security is another good example for skills and a learning plan. Security is something that DBAs do every day with access controls. There are also audit tools in place to pull activities on the databases, but there could be a need for other activity monitoring tools or writing skills development for policies and security baselines. New skills would be a mark with just a "Learn" in Figure 10-2, but increasing knowledge in a skill will be both know and learn.

Acquiring

We learned that the cloud environment provides a great sandbox for testing and exploring the cloud environment. Hands-On training is critical for the technical skill set that is needed.

Where else to acquire the desired skills? There are plenty of options, but let me suggest a few:

- User Communities – IOUG for Cloud, Data Services, Analytics and Integrations, DMA. There are also security communities for the security.

- Formal Training – This could be a week-long course that is focused on the skill.

- Conferences – Vendor conferences such as Oracle and Microsoft will have conferences on their cloud and other database skills.

- On the Job – Again this can use the cloud environments, understanding of the existing environment, and from coworkers.

Mentoring

Through the user group communities or work there is potential to learn from each other. Sharing ideas of how to architect or design a migration to the cloud could be extremely helpful: for example, having others either work through this transformation together or having the experience to partner up with those just getting started with the transition.

A person to discuss if they have seen something in the environment before like that or would plan A or plan B be better, and of course they are going to come back with plan C.

If anyone has mentored a Junior or New DBA, they realize the value in this. Much more is received from the relationship than what is put into it. It does take more than one person to make these environments work as designed.

This is important for leadership potential and develops communication and relationship building skills. Understand that it is important to be selective when it comes to mentoring. It can be through a full-out mentorship program or just a few people exchanging information to network and keep in touch as needed.

What Stays the Same

This might have been better in the last chapter, but there are a few things that comfort us when they stay the same. Not everything can change at once.

Data is data, and it will continue to grow. Because of this, data professionals should always be able to find careers. There are also careers in technology that will be available for those that continue to learn.

Figure 10-3 shows just a quick look at what is staying the same. There are going to be support and operational teams with production and test environments that we will be dealing with. It might also become an area for change further down in the future but for now this is staying the same.

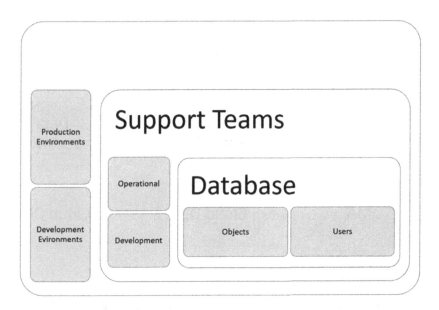

Figure 10-3. *Things that stay the same*

Not Just a DBA

Hopefully after this discussion, this is a statement that is removed from your vocabulary. There are no longer just DBAs and at the minimum DBAs are also administering cloud databases. There are quite a few options and career path choices to make.

Figure 10-4 has the possible organizational structure of the "C" offices. This is to give you an idea of a career path and potential as well. The DBAs under CDO and CSO are more in the role of application DBA as the DBA might now be the role of supporting the application or even the cloud.

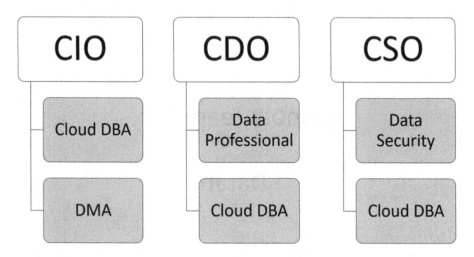

Figure 10-4. *Career paths*

There are a couple of different options to put in the Cloud DBA and Data Security, but this is a more typical model and just serves as a reminder of not only the technical roles and how it fits in the organizational model. There are possibilities for CIO, CDO, and CSO development, and why not, especially since the data is a very valuable commodity to the business. A person who can understand that, where it belongs in the organization, and use it for driving decisions is a strong force and valuable asset themselves in the company.

DBAs are adaptive and are constantly learning. The environments that they support can be on-premise, in the cloud, or both, but this will not matter as the DBA is now taking a look at what needs to be done for skills to manage their transformation just like they are planning migrations to the cloud or consolidations.

Conclusion

The landscape of the databases has changed. The technology developments and having cloud computing and on-demand services is increasing the challenges of for the DBA. There needs to be a transformation of the DBA to reach new levels. They already possess valuable skills with database knowledge and business processes.

The key is leveraging the existing skills and meet this challenge head-on, increasing their knowledge in cloud and data processes. There is such growth potential with the on-demand service for the DBAs. In developing DBaaS, the DBA can provide the tools to run levels of security or other configurations to build it into the service. On-Demand and Cloud Computing allow the DBAs to work more with developers and applications teams.

The career growth as a DBA requires a shift, transition to adjust course, and leverage current skills with new ones. You can decide which path you would prefer to take and build out a plan to enhance and acquire new skills.

The job of the DBA is one that very rarely has the same day twice. The DBAs are evolving out of technology disruptors. It is an interesting time to be part of the data profession as the amount of data is enormous, and all of the sources coming will continue to make this a fast and growing system.

DBAs hold the opportunity to transform into an area they want to and are excited about. Remember, security is also an option too and especially plays into some of the natural skills. DBA transformation is going to happen with the movement of the database to cloud, automation, and on-demand services.

Index

A

Addressing vulnerabilities, 79
Application DBAs, 8
Application Program Interfaces
    (APIs), 37, 38
Application *vs.* Cloud DBA, 65
Artificial Intelligence (AI), 34
Auditing, 77
Augmented Reality (AR), 34
Authentication, 73
Authorization, 73
Automation DBAs
    code automation, 11
    dependencies, 96
    monitoring, 11
    schedule, 11
    security, 78
    tasks, 94
    test plans, 96

B

Big data, 89
Business intelligence, 90

C

Capacity planning, Cloud DBA, 60
Change management, 104

Chief Cloud Officer (CCO), 4
Chief Data Officer (CDO), 3, 83
Chief Security Officer (CSO), 4
Cisco Virtual Networking, 28
Cloud Appliance, 47
Cloud computing, 12, 53, 119
Cloud databases, 38
Cloud database tasks, 57
Cloud DBAs
    vs. applications, 65
    capacity planning, 60
    Cloud Control, 59
    creation of, 58
    data analysis, 62
    data migration, 63
    vs. DBaaS, 67
    discovering, 61
    evaluation, 112
    security features, 63
    tasks, 56
    tools, 59
    types of, 53
    workload analysis, 62
Cloud Engineered System, 47
Cloud providers, 40, 41, 64, 77,
    102, 103
Cloud security, 76
Cloud Service Models, 55, 66

Cloud therapy, 101
Code automation, 11
Common Vulnerability Scoring
        System (CVSS), 79
Container database (CDB), 6
Cyber Security
        Framework, 72

D

Database administration (DBA)
    application, 8
    automation, 10
    career paths, 118
    defined, 3
    high availability, 7
    infratructure, 6
    manageability, 7
    recovery, 7
    skill set, 13, 111
    soft skills, 17
    storage, 7
    system, 5
    technical skills, 14
Database administrators
    job satisfaction, 100
    skill development, 107
Database as a Service (DBaaS)
    APIs, 37, 38
    vs. cloud DBA, 67
    definition, 36–37
    design and
        advantages, 38
Database creation, 58, 66

Database Machine
        Administrator (DMA)
    appliances, 46
    automation, 49
    Cloud Engineered System, 47
    control of, 50
    design and architecture
        decisions, 49
    evaluation, 112
    Exadata Database Machine, 44
    SuperCluster, 47
Database objects, 8, 21
Database platform, 36
Database security
    addressing vulnerabilities, 79
    auditing, 77
    DBA teams, 72
    evaluation, 112
    reducing risk, 74
    reporting, 77
    security learning, 80–81
    security planning, 72–74
    security team, 69–71
Database servers, 7
Database technology
    data types, 31
    storage, 30
Data collection, 27, 89, 91
Data flows, 21–22
Data integrations, 22, 88
Data management, 9
Data migrations, 9, 65
Data modeling, 8
Data ownership, 102

Data professionals, 83, 112
Data protection, 63, 73
Data quality
    classification, 87
    development
        process, 84–85
    and governance, 86
    MDM, 84, 85
Data retention, 102
Data Warehouse, 28
Data workflows, 83
Disk operations, 31
Disruptors
    security, 33
    social networking, 33
    technology, 33

E, F

Enterprise Cloud Control, 50
Enterprise database, 35
Enterprise thinking, 71
Exadata Database Machine, 44
Extract, load, transform (ETL)
    processes, 88

G

General Data Protection
    Regulation (GDPR), 74

H

Hybrid clouds, 54

I, J, K

Identity theft, 86
Infrastructure as a Service (IaaS),
    40
Interpersonal skills, 21

L

Leadership
    developing skills, 25
    team building, 24
    team goals, 25

M

Massively Parallel Processing
    (MPP) databases, 89
Master Data Management (MDM),
    84, 85
Mentoring, 115
Microsoft SQL Server, 6
Mobile Data Traffic, 29

N

National Vulnerability
    Database, 79

O

On-demand services, 37, 39, 119
Oracle 12c, 6
Oracle Cloud, 39, 47, 59, 63, 98, 107

Oracle Cloud Manager, 10
Oracle Data Integrator (ODI), 88
Oracle Enterprise Cloud
    Control, 59
Oracle Enterprise Manager, 10
Oracle Exadata engineered
    systems, 30
Oracle machine offerings, 49
Organizational chart, 3–4

P, Q

Password management, 73
Performance tuning, 9
Platform as a Service (PaaS), 40
Pluggable databases (PDB), 6
Privacy, 102
Private clouds, 47, 54–55
Public cloud, 54, 55, 61

R

Real Application
    Clusters (RAC), 7, 44
Real Application Testing (RAT), 97

S

Security Information and Event
    Management (SIEM), 78
Security learning, 80
Security planning, 72–74
Security teams, 69–71

Server OS, 50
Service-level agreements, 102
Service-oriented architecture, 106
Skill learning plan, 114
Social networking, 33
Soft skills
    adaptability, 21
    communication, 18
    documentation, 20
    leadership, 23
    organizational, 22
    relationship
        building, 21
Software as a Service (SaaS), 40
Solid State Disks (SSD), 31
Standardization security
    in Cloud, 76
SuperCluster, 47
Systems DBA, 5

T

Technical skills
    Core *vs.* Oracle, 15
    installs and upgrades, 17
    platform-specific, 14
    testing and implementation, 17
Test environment, 107
Transformation plan
    acquiring, 115
    DBA skills, 110–112
    evaluation, 112
    planning, 113

U

Unit testing, 97

V

Virtualization, 47
Virtual reality (VR), 34

Vulnerabilities
 addressing, 79
 and risks, 74

W, X, Y, Z

Work-life balance, 105
Workload analysis, 62

Get the eBook for only $5!

Why limit yourself?

With most of our titles available in both PDF and ePUB format, you can access your content wherever and however you wish—on your PC, phone, tablet, or reader.

Since you've purchased this print book, we are happy to offer you the eBook for just $5.

To learn more, go to http://www.apress.com/companion or contact support@apress.com.

Apress®

For the Complete Technology & Database Professional

IOUG represents the **voice of Oracle technology and database professionals** - empowering you to be **more productive** in your business and career by **delivering education,** sharing **best practices** and providing technology direction and **networking opportunities.**

Context, Not Just Content

IOUG is dedicated to helping our members become an #IOUGenius by staying on the cutting-edge of Oracle technologies and industry issues through practical content, user-focused education, and invaluable networking and leadership opportunities:

- *SELECT Journal* is our quarterly publication that provides in-depth, peer-reviewed articles on industry news and best practices in Oracle technology

- Our #IOUGenius blog highlights a featured weekly topic and provides content driven by Oracle professionals and the IOUG community

- Special Interest Groups provide you the chance to collaborate with peers on the specific issues that matter to you and even take on leadership roles outside of your organization

- COLLABORATE is our once-a-year opportunity to connect with the members of not one, but three, Oracle users groups (IOUG, OAUG and Quest) as well as with the top names and faces in the Oracle community.

Who we are...

... **more than 20,000** database professionals, developers, application and infrastructure architects, business intelligence specialists and IT managers

... **a community of users** that share experiences and knowledge on issues and technologies that matter to you and your organization

Interested? Join IOUG's community of Oracle technology and database professionals at www.ioug.org/Join.

Independent Oracle Users Group | phone: (312) 245-1579 | email: membership@ioug.org
330 N. Wabash Ave., Suite 2000, Chicago, IL 60611

Printed in the United States
By Bookmasters